D0429695

EAGLE VALLEY LIBRARY DISTRICT
P.O. BOX 240 600 BROADWAY
EAGLE, CO 81631 / 328-8800

JAMerica

ALSO BY PETER CONNERS

Nonfiction

Growing Up Dead:
  The Hallucinated Confessions of a Teenage Deadhead

White Hand Society:
  The Psychedelic Partnership of Timothy Leary & Allen Ginsberg

Poetry

The Crows Were Laughing in Their Trees

Of Whiskey and Winter

Fiction

Emily Ate the Wind

PP/FF: An Anthology (editor)

JAMerica

The History of the Jam Band and Festival Scene

from the Grateful Dead to Phish,

from H.O.R.D.E. to Bonnaroo, and Beyond

Peter Conners

DA CAPO PRESS
A Member of the Perseus Books Group

Copyright © 2013 by Peter Conners

All rights reserved. No part of this publication may be reproduced, stored in a re-
trieval system, or transmitted, in any form or by any means, electronic, mechanical,
photocopying, recording, or otherwise, without the prior written permission of the
publisher. Printed in the United States of America. For information, address Da Capo
Press, 44 Farnsworth Street, 3rd Floor, Boston, MA 02210.

Designed by Jeff Williams
Set in 12 point Fairfield LT by The Perseus Books Group

Library of Congress Cataloging-in-Publication Data

Conners, Peter H.
    AMerica: the history of the jam band and festival scene / Peter Conners.
      pages cm
   Includes bibliographical references and index.
      ISBN 978-0-306-82066-3 (hardcover)—ISBN 978-0-306-82239-1 (e-book)
 1. Jam bands—United States—History. 2. Musicians—United States—Interviews.
 3. Popular music—United States—History and criticism. I. Title.

ML3477.C665 2013
781.64078'73—dc23

                                                                        2013012646

First Da Capo Press edition 2013

Published by Da Capo Press
A Member of the Perseus Books Group
www.dacapopress.com

Da Capo Press books are available at special discounts for bulk purchases in the U.S.
by corporations, institutions, and other organizations. For more information, please
contact the Special Markets Department at the Perseus Books Group, 2300 Chest-
nut Street, Suite 200, Philadelphia, PA 19103, or call (800) 810-4145, ext. 5000, or
e-mail special.markets@perseusbooks.com.

10 9 8 7 6 5 4 3 2 1

For the roadies, the crew, the staff
with the "Work" laminates who bring the music to the stage

Contents

Preface

JAMerica: The State of the Union

LET'S GET THIS OUT OF THE WAY. I apologize in advance to any bands who feel themselves unfairly lumped into the jam band category as a result of this book. Personally, I sympathize completely with an artist not wanting to be pigeonholed. The tools, the instruments, the genres, and traditions are all there—why settle for limiting yourself within prefab borders?

The flipside is that "jam band" is a tremendously useful label when used responsibly. It is not, however, useful as shorthand for concert or album reviews that prematurely write off the work under consideration as throwback hippie music. It is never useful when accompanied by the adjective "noodling." Hippies and noodling are lazy signifiers tossed up to fill in the vacuum of word-count deadlines. I have never once seen a worthwhile guitar player "noodle." And I saw the Grateful Dead. A lot. To describe a guitarist's technique as noodling is to throw up your hands and retreat from a deeper layer of guitar playing. Those "noodling" players usually have ear-melting chops and musical knowledge that inevitably leads to improvisational playing, a chance to test those skills by chasing them far enough into the unknown that you can start driving them back again through an elusive, shape-shifting soundscape.

At the core of all jam bands is a dedication to improvisation as a chance to create a unique, spontaneous, artistic/musical event shared between band and artist. A jam band cannot reach that point without the energy of the audience. Nor can the audience reach it without the band. That chance to "go there" and "get off" on the music is the product of a shared agreement between the band and the fan. That singular, shared musical experience is the beating heart of the jam band scene.

Unfortunately, the jam band label has too often been used as a scalpel to cut out that beating heart. So let's begin by breaking away from a one-dimensional view of the term and look at the characteristics these so-called jam bands share:

1) Dedication to creating a singular musical event shared by band and audience generally driven by improvisational moments.

1.a.) My instinct is to state that a certain level of musicianship is necessary to be considered a jam band. The truth is that many jam band musicians are the best schooled (formally or informally) and experienced (road tested) you'll find outside of an orchestra pit. However—and particularly in the Americana strain of jam band under which I'd include Donna the Buffalo and Railroad Earth—there is affection for the less polished, rougher-hewn, homemade, or "old time" sound. In describing Donna the Buffalo, David Gans sums up this ethos nicely in his interview: "No pretense of instrumental virtuosity, no shredding solos, no wankery whatsoever—just a deep, deep, deep groove and spiritually positive songs that make you glad to be alive and an audience that's all right there with you." In these cases overt shows of musicianship would only detract from the larger performance. That said, we must also acknowledge the severe vocal limits many jam band singers suffer from. They eek out a "ragged but right" way through their vocals by creating their own signature squawks and squalls, and the music becomes intertwined with—if not defined by—these limitations. But these limitations can also leave many jam bands sounding amateurish and, thus, open to criticism of their overall musicianship. Ironically some of the weakest vocals can come from the most skilled musicians. In the end, other than an ability to improvise, it's best not to assume a specific level of musicianship when constructing a jam band definition.

2) Emphasis on live performance over recorded works. Bands that encourage taping of their performances reinforce this focus.

3) Conscious effort by the band to connect with a grassroots following of fans. This, naturally, implies reciprocity in the fans' effort to connect; however, that type of connection appears in every genre of music. The difference in the jam scene is that the fans become a vitally important part of experiencing the band; symbols, rituals, slang, and esoteric history become tickets to fully understanding the band itself. In the process the fans become so closely identified with the band that they often evolve their own names (e.g., Deadheads, Phishheads, The Herd, Spreadheads, etc.) that, simultaneously, link them to the band, make them a more coherent group, and begin to define the individuals even outside of the musical realm.

All of the bands included in this book are, according to my definition, either jam bands or central to the jam band story. Over the two years it took to conduct these interviews I met almost no musicians who embrace that label without reservation. In fact, many made it clear at the outset that they either wanted to distance themselves from the label or had only grudgingly accepted it. There were certainly a handful of bands and artists—perhaps even your favorites—that declined (always through their management) to be interviewed for this book despite being clearly associated with the jam band scene. Was that a result of wanting to distance themselves from the "jam band" label? In some cases, yes, that was my impression. Whatever the reason, if your favorite jam band isn't interviewed here, there's a good chance it wasn't for lack of trying. But as is always the case in jam band land, the show must go on. In cases in which I felt that the band or artist was inevitable as part of a jam band discussion, excerpts of previously published interviews were inserted into *JAMerica*. All of those instances are noted, and acknowledgments have been provided. Otherwise, all interviews are new and conducted expressly for this book.

As a result of the tension around the jam band label, I felt it was fair and accurate to expand *JAMerica*'s premise to include the term "festival band." Jam bands play a lot of music festivals: Mountain Jam in Hunter, New York; Hangout Music Festival in Gulf Shores, Alabama; All Good Music Festival in Thornville, Ohio; Gathering of the Vibes in Bridgeport, Connecticut; High Sierra Music Festival in Quincy, California—far too many to compile here, including the floating Jam Cruise. In some cases bands have organized their own annual festivals, sometimes even named after themselves (e.g., the band moe. has a yearly "moe.down") or named after their fans (e.g., the Disco Biscuits' "Camp Bisco"). It is not hard to trace these festivals back to that weary sixties touchstone, Woodstock, that signifies everything these bands fear they'll be dismissed as once pegged as jam bands. But as of this writing, there is no stigma associated with being a festival band.

In these pages you will hear people struggling with the "jam band" label. It will be pushed, pulled, shunned, and derided despite the fact that it has now been an accurate descriptor for two decades. In an early phone call with Tara Nevins from Donna the Buffalo, she ultimately conceded that because her band was regularly lumped in as a jam band, this book might be helpful in getting a handle around what that term actually means. That's as close to the animating spirit of this book as I can imagine.

MY FIRST GLIMPSE of the emerging jam band scene came in the fall of 1989 during my freshman year at SUNY Potsdam. By the time I got there I had been to a few dozen Dead shows and was determined that my schooling not interfere with seeing a few dozen more. Grades be damned, that was the way it went down too. However, a few other things happened along the way. Most importantly, I met my lifelong friend, musician, and longtime staple of the Colorado music scene, Todd Weiner. Todd had been trained on multiple instruments, but his main passion was the drums. Unfortunately he wasn't allowed to practice his drums in the dorm rooms. So when we became roommates Todd played more and more guitar and began teaching me how to play too. He also started playing in a band called Fathead Minnow.

Whenever Fathead Minnow rehearsed I was in the corner of the room watching how a group of individual musicians transforms into a band. As soon as they started gigging around Potsdam I became their roadie, assistant soundman, and number-one fan. For the first time I got to see how a band works from the inside while also learning more about music through my own fledgling guitar studies. This all deepened my passion for the Grateful Dead.

However, it also opened me up to the possibility that smaller, up-start bands could replicate the Grateful Dead's musical, social, and business model.

Fathead Minnow was a jam band in every sense of the term. Along with covers of the Dead, Bob Dylan, Jimi Hendrix, and so forth along with a handful of originals, they also played covers from new bands like Phish, Widespread Panic, and Blues Traveler. The reality is that Fathead Minnow was covering Phish songs shortly after Phish wrote them. We dubbed and passed around copies of *Lawnboy* by Phish, *Space Wrangler* by Widespread Panic, and a demo tape by Blues Traveler that ended up making up a chunk of their self-titled debut album. Over time these bands were joined by Aquarium Rescue Unit, the Spin Doctors, the Authority, and many of the other bands referenced, if not interviewed, in this book. In short, the jam band scene was blossoming and, as op-posed to the San Francisco-based burgeoning of the psychedelic scene twenty-five years earlier, upstate New York was a great van-tage point. There were amazing club shows happening all over the East Coast, and oftentimes bands shared stages with each other. In the summer of 1991 I went to a small musical festival at Arrow-head Ranch in the Catskill Mountains featuring the Spin Doc-tors, the Authority, TR3, Aquarium Rescue Unit, the Radiators, and Phish. The fact that something new was happening—that the scene the Grateful Dead had pioneered was morphing into this next phase—was apparent everywhere. We weren't new converts to this scene playing catch-up on twenty-five years of history we'd missed; this was our scene, and it was starting from scratch.

Twenty years later that process has played itself out through subsequent "generations" of jam bands. Like some amplified biblical parable, the Grateful Dead and the Allman Brothers be-gat Phish and Widespread Panic who begat moe. and the String Cheese Incident who begat. . . . Interestingly the scene has continued long enough that people now associate Warren Haynes with Gov't Mule instead of the Allman Brothers, and members of the Grateful Dead can be seen playing with kids who were mere toddlers when Jerry Garcia died. At the time of this writing the jam band scene is richer, more diverse, and bigger than ever. Every region has its own music festival, where musical improvisation is the expectation and tapers' microphone stands poke out of the grass like porcupine quills. Instead of fuzzy bootleg tapes, live shows are posted online and links are e-mailed around the country before the last drum is packed into its carrying case. The Internet was custom made for the jam band scene and has been a tremendous boon to this grassroots-driven culture.

The state of the union is strong.

One recurring theme that came up during these interviews was the distance between jam bands and the corporate music industry. Because jam bands have never relied on record sales for their primary income, they were largely unfazed when corporate record sales took a nosedive. Not only that, but in making their music available through downloads and viewing album sales as only one piece of their larger business plan, they were ahead of the curve in the industry's response to those lagging sales. The fact is that aside from a few classic albums by the progenitors of the modern jam band scene (the Allman Brothers' *At Fillmore East* and *Eat a Peach* come immediately to mind), the music industry and the jam band scene have seldom bothered interacting. There are many reasons for that, but one major reason is the fact that jam music has never been associated with a single geographical area. Traditionally, the music industry has colonized "hot cities," turning them into the newest "it" places for breaking bands. But with jam there is no geography to colonize; instead, the bands colonize the geography. They are constantly in motion, absorbing styles from around the country and distilling it through hard-to-classify amalgamations of genre-hyphenated music. Perhaps that's one reason the jam scene has largely eluded the corporate harvesting visited upon so many cities. Jam isn't about geography or the fashion that inevitably accompanies it. Outside of pure documentation, it is not camera friendly or "ready for its close-up." It is aural, and if it is photogenic at all, those lenses are best focused on the audience rather than the bands. Simply put: it's hard to hit a moving target. And if there is one trait that jam bands have in common, it is being moving targets.

Most music-based oral histories focus on either a single band or on the development of a musical "scene" within a city that went on to become famous for a particular style of music (I'm looking at you, Seattle). However, unlike grunge, jam music isn't a quick burst on the public consciousness, complete with fashion, a central record label (Sub Pop being the main progenitors of the "Seattle sound"), and a location to pin it on. Depending on who you ask, jam music has been around for anywhere from twenty years to the prehistoric ages. It has kept largely out of the spotlight, quietly growing itself in nurturing pockets around the country where the bands were able to garner early audiences and develop their music before taking it on the road. Once on the road they often played with similarly minded bands in those bands' home cities, thus broadening the fan-base for both bands. The jam scene is cooperative to the brink of being incestuous—and I mean that in the best way. However, to create a semblance of coherence, I needed to lay some parameters on the development of the jam band scene.

It's true that the origins of the jam band scene are most strongly rooted in the counterculture bands of the 1960s, most notably the Grateful Dead. However, for the purposes of this book, those bands—and that band in particular—fall under the category of "models and inspirations" for the contemporary jam band scene rather than members. As you will see, there isn't a band in this book who wouldn't acknowledge some debt to the Grateful Dead. It's no reach to say that with no Grateful Dead, there would be no jam band scene. But the larger jam band scene was grown by the subsequent generation of musicians and fans who took note of the band's music, history, and modes of operation and adapted them for their own purposes. The jam band story belongs to those individuals.

THE JAM BAND and festival scene was launched on America in 1992 under the auspices of the cumbersomely named rock festival Horizons of Rock Developing Everywhere. The festival is commonly referred to by its acronym, H.O.R.D.E. The first incarnation of H.O.R.D.E is a roll call of the fathers of the jam and festival scene: Blues Traveler, Widespread Panic, the Spin Doctors, Aquarium Rescue Unit, and Phish. Interestingly all of these bands also played the previous summer at the short-lived musical Shangri-La known as Arrowhead Ranch.

On July 21 and 22, 1991, Phish headlined Arrowhead Ranch supported by the Spin Doctors, the Radiators, the Authority, and TR3. That same summer Blues Traveler took the Arrowhead stage along with Widespread Panic and the Dreyer Brothers. As with all of these bands—and nearly every band I interviewed—the Arrowhead scene was inspired by the Grateful Dead. The lineup of bands playing there during 1990 and 1991 reflects that. The most direct connection is the appearance of Gratefully Yours, who played there on August 25, 1991, featuring Papa John Creach, former Grateful Dead keyboardist Tom (T. C.) Constanten, and such Dead compatriots and fellow musicians as David Nelson, Steve Kimock, and longtime Jerry Garcia sideman Merl Saunders. Other musicians who played Arrowhead during 1990–1991 include Max Creek, Richie Havens, Hot Tuna, New Riders of the Purple Sage, and Kingfish. There are no more than two degrees (and, in most cases, one) of separation between all of these bands and the Grateful Dead. However, the closest connection is less obvious: that landmark series of shows during the summer of 1991 was organized in part by a fledgling music promoter with incredibly deep music roots—David Graham. David's father, San Francisco–based music impresario Bill Graham, was known affectionately by Deadheads (and much to his chagrin) as Uncle Bobo. Although many who dealt with him know Graham as a fierce, unrelenting businessman, former Grateful Dead keyboardist Tom Constanten recalls in his JAMerica interview that "Bill had a gentle, considerate side which he hardly ever showed to the public. Sometimes at band meetings you would see his thoughtfulness come out. He would say things like, 'Don't tell anyone I said this, but . . .' Jerry Garcia had a great point about Bill Graham. He said, 'If he really was the scoundrel that some people made him out to be, he could have gotten a lot richer a lot faster than by making work for musicians.'"

It is impossible to overstate the role that Bill Graham played in promoting the 1960s counterculture bands that shaped today's jam scene. Graham's connection to the Grateful Dead is a constant touchstone in the band's history. If he had done nothing in the music industry besides found the Fillmore West and East, he would still be a legend. However, Graham did much more. One of his final acts in fostering the music scene that he had helped create was to encourage his son's interest in the nascent jam scene (mainly Blues Traveler, who David managed), which in turn flowered into the Arrowhead shows of 1991. If not for his tragic death in a helicopter crash in October 1991, who knows how Bill Graham could have used his experience and clout to usher the scene to its next incarnation? But with Uncle Bobo gone, it was left to the bands and their equally green crews and management to pick up where Arrowhead left off. As a widely touring band and also central figures in the New York City jam scene, where all of the

Arrowhead and H.O.R.D.E. bands played at one time or another (usually at Wetlands Preserve), Blues Traveler, led by the intrepid, ever-feisty John Popper, were in a solid place to keep the energy from the summer of 1991 going into a new venture that would send the hungry jam band scene stumbling into the world.

"We Wanted to
Call It Lollapatchouli"

David Graham: I guess the way I originally got into it was the spring of '89. I was at Columbia University, and a bunch of my friends went to a show at Barnard College, which is across the street. There was this little grass courtyard, and a band was setting up—forty or fifty people sitting on the ground, very mellow scene, nice weekend day in New York. All of a sudden Popper started to blow some notes, and it was like the Pied Piper was playing and everyone just stood up like someone was blowing a human dog whistle. Then the band kicked in and everyone freaked out for like three hours. That was my introduction to Blues Traveler. From that moment on I caught wind of what was going on in the city. The Spin Doctors' guys played in the bottom of our basement in a fraternity in New York. Some people say they played their first gig with those four members in our basement. I don't know if it's true, though. I forget which one came before the other one, but those were the two things that introduced me to the local scene. Then once I got to become friendly with Traveler I started going to the

Nightingale, and they played all sorts of venues, and eventually the Wetlands became the go-to place.

Chris Barron: We were looking for places to play. We were playing stuff that nobody knew or wanted to hear. There were kids who wanted to hear the stuff we were playing, but they hadn't really heard it yet. Then there were the people who ran the clubs, and it's like, "What the hell is this shit?" They would say, "Um, no, you can't play here." In the beginning we would make our own gigs. So we would find some place that would let us use the space, and we would come up with some nefarious stuff for people to eat or drink and just fill some weird room with freaks freaking and just play music for them.

Jono Manson: It was a very fertile time in terms of live music in New York. Coming out of the late seventies into the early eighties with the whole, like, punk and, you know, new wave and all that . . . all of a sudden there was a resurgence of live music clubs. And then there was a whole rockabilly revival and all these kind of moves back towards roots music. And there was always a handful of blues clubs in New York. Like, there was a place just down the street from the Nightingale called Dan Lynch, which was sort of a real . . . the only real sort of roadhouse blues bar that had been there. It was an old Irish bar that had turned into a music club. And at the time that Nightingale—which was on the same block—opened, Dan Lynch had been established for at least a decade at that point. Probably since the midseventies I think it started. I was in a band called the Worms, which was, um, despite our name, was really just a roots rock band. We played—it was an all-original band—but we played sort of jump blues style. Well, we actually played almost every style. And our shows would sort of flow one thing into the next. In that sense we were kind of a jam band. Although a lot of the bands on that scene at the time weren't jam bands necessarily in the sense that people think of today. In any case this bar, the Nightingale, was down the street, and they had no live music. And I remember the owner of the place stopped into Dan Lynch's one night when we were playing there and said, "I'd like to start having music in my club. Would you come check it out?" So myself and a couple of the other guys from my band walked into the place, and it was just a dump. Just a dive bar. And we looked around the place and said, "Perfect. This is great."

John Popper: The beginning of it was when we came to New York City, that Nightingale scene that Jono was, in my mind, king of. We got very into the New York scene, then suddenly started to seem a little different! There was this sort of hippie scene, and we fit right into that.

Jono Manson: The guy was basically saying, "Look, I've seen you guys play. I've seen some of the other bands that are part of your sort of family of groups, and I want you to come in here and do what you like." And at first he didn't even pay the bands, you know. We played in there and passed the hat. But we were willing to do that because we saw the opportunity to create something of our own. We were all young bands. And back then, during that time, lots of little clubs were springing up. I mean, I had years in the early- to mideighties where I played over 365 gigs a year without leaving New York City. Just by virtue of the fact that some days we'd play from eight to ten at one joint and then go play from eleven until four in the morning at another place. So more than one gig a day, four, five days a week, and it would add up to more than 365 gigs a year, without leaving the five boroughs of New York—without barely leaving Manhattan, because the whole Brooklyn scene and everything that's going on now, that was . . . it was rare that we would do gigs in Brooklyn. Anyways, so that's kind of how that scene started. And there was a growing interest in live music and particularly blues and roots music, that kind of stuff. I would say that set the stage for what then turned into the jam band revival. And younger bands, like Blues Traveler, would come over. For example, I remember the night I met Joan Osborne, who was also part of our family. Although she came up, she came later. And I remember, you know, she came into the Nightingale one night and walked up to me and Jerry Dugger, who was the bass player in the Worms, and said, "My name is Joan, and I want to be a singer." And she started working the open mics and there was . . . most of these clubs would have an open mic night, but the quality of the musicianship was really high at the time—there were so many great players around, and there was so much opportunity. And we were all getting paid. And then the Nightingale turned into actually a . . . I mean it was a dump, it was a teeny little bar, but once we developed the scene there, then we started charging a cover at the door. We had a doorman. And the bands got the lion's share of the money. And we were making, as far as bar band money, you know, four or five times as much as bands are making now for playing a similar venue. And that's twenty-five years ago. Longer even than twenty-five years ago. It was the early 1980s I'm talking about. Rent on my apartment in Park Slope was five hundred bucks a month. So I was paying my rent easily. We were all working and making money. So I think that is one of the keys, too, to the scene happening. People were working and feeling appreciated in every way—you know, also financially. Now it's a lot harder for younger bands coming up in little scenes like that to really make a living at it.

Stephen Robinson: In the then-brand-new second-generation jam scene, two of the main acts were Blues Traveler and Spin

Doctors. Both of those bands had come up out of playing at two venues in New York City: Wetlands and the very small Nightingale, located at 213 2nd Avenue, at the corner of 2nd Avenue and 13th Street—significant numbers for any Deadhead, particularly me, who was born on that historic day—February 13, 1970—when the Dead played one of the most famous shows they ever played. Every band in the jam scene wanted to play those venues, and it was an honor for us to play them both.

Jono Manson: Blues Traveler, I remember when they first started playing at the Nightingale. They were doing opening slots on weekend nights with some of the more established bands that were on the scene. My group was there. There was another band called the Surreal McCoys, who were . . . again, we were jam bands in the sense that one song would sometimes flow into the next, and we would extend things out. But it wasn't, you know, jam band in the sense of, like . . . you couldn't really trace our lineage from the Grateful Dead and that whole line of the tree. We were more influenced by the same things that those guys were influenced by, you know. But still it was a natural progression of things. Then bands like Blues Traveler started showing up on the scene. And younger people started coming. Those clubs were all downtown, the NYU kids—all the college kids would come. And it was a very mixed crowd. You had, you know, the blues and R&B. The audience for that is wide ranging in age. Especially now—it's an older audience. But the younger bands, the teenage bands were coming in. I mean I was in my midtwenties then, but the difference . . . when you're in your twenties the difference in age between you and someone who's seventeen seems gigantic. So those bands were coming in, and the demographic of the audience started to change, and the younger kids were coming with their marijuana, and, uh, that scene started to grow. Also around the same time Spin Doctors started to play, and they had a . . . they used to hold Monday nights at the Nightingale for a long time, which was the crappiest night of the week. And they would pack the place. You know, it was mostly the NYU kids. And so that's where a lot of those bands really developed their following.

Chris Barron: Yeah, well, the thing that was great about that, when you think about it, the thing with Nightingale, it was more happening outside than it was inside. Inside you're in there with the band and that was great, there was great music happening, but it's like a shit hole. *Shit hole*. God knows what they were doing. Supposedly, the thing that was amazing, from my understanding of the whole Nightingale thing, the phenomenon in the Nightingale was they didn't really need to make any money. So Tom H., who had nothing to do with anything going on—just booking the bands—he was just standing at the door doing music, nothing else to do with anything else that was going on. But they didn't care if they made money. . . .

Jono Manson: The Nightingale itself was a drug bar. I mean, there was a house coke dealer in the bar. Remember, this was the eighties in New York City—the whole age of excess. There was a certain early evening clientele. There was a coke dealer that went on duty, every night, at 6 p.m. If you came to the Nightingale around quarter to six, you'd see a lot of Wall Street guys, and they'd be nervously hanging around, waiting for this guy (whose name I won't mention, because to the best of my knowledge he's still a free man) to show up. All of a sudden there's a guy in the bar every night at 6 p.m. selling, like, massive quantities of blow to whoever wants to come in there. You gotta wonder if there aren't greater forces at work. But none of us ever really questioned it, you know. And yeah, some of the musicians befriended these types who actually were very grateful at the masses that we brought in. It was a very different time than today in terms of . . . you know, you could smoke pot in the bar. People would light up during a show. So there were drugs, for sure.

Chris Barron: Tom could book anything he wanted to. Tom could be this impresario, and he didn't need any financial motivations necessarily. He made more money when bands brought more people, but somehow he didn't seem to give a shit really whether you brought a lot of people. If you didn't bring anybody, he'd keep booking you. Spin Doctors, Blues Traveler—there were nights in there where there was only, like, eleven people, and four of them were our girlfriends and two more were our girlfriends' friends, and a couple people who actually wanted to see the band. But they stuck with us. Tom stuck with us, and we started building something up. But eventually, when it was superpacked in there, it was like a festival, sort of. It was like our Monday night festival, the cool place to be. I'd go and see Blues Traveler, and I'd seen them innumerable times, so I didn't go in until I heard them do "Gloria" and I knew it was my turn to get up and do a scat solo with Popper. But it was just as fun outside 'cause people were smoking funny cigarettes and passing a paper bag of something. It was just a whole party that was going on outside.

David Graham: It was quite a scene. I have lived in New York, and I know that music scenes come and go in the city, and this was a very vibrant time for music—and it was cool. The musicians loved playing together. They would jam in and out of each other. The Spin Doctors and Traveler in the early years were very linked up, and also the people who worked with the bands.

Jono Manson: There was a real sense of collaboration, of family, of togetherness as opposed to competition. And that's something that's the rarest and most precious element of what was going on then. It was this real sense of collaboration, and nobody felt like they were competing against the other one for their gig. Or like, "Oh well, you got Tuesday night—I wanted Tuesday night." As a matter of fact, we would be waiting to get off one gig so we could go sit in with somebody else in another place down the street. I mean, the Nightingale—I think the official capacity was like eighty people and we'd have three hundred–something in there. The bar was maybe like thirty feet away, and when you're done playing a set it took you like half an hour to go get a drink at the bar because there was just so much humanity packed in there. And literally I remember the ceiling—the walls and ceiling—would drip with people's sweat, like going off into the air. It was great!

There's something really cool about the home scene, in, like, a homegrown scene, and, you know, it eventually has to grow. So you lose some of that innocence, the energy of that time, and trade it for something that's more inclusive and that brings in other influences. I think the same thing even happened to the Nightingale scene, where bands from outside of the city were catching wind, "Well this is a dump." I mean the same with CBGB. Nightingale was to roots rock and the jam band scene what CBGBs was to the punk scene. You know, every punk band . . . I mean CBGBs was a dump too, you know, but that's where you had to go, that's where you had to play. Bands were willing—bands were clamoring—to be on a bill with five other bands and not get paid and get screamed at by Hilly the owner because that was the thing to do. The Nightingale became seen that way, whether correctly or incorrectly, by a lot of young bands from out of town, who then started wanting to get booked there. And that did also change the vibe. And then in the next level is the Wetlands.

Jeff Mattson: The band [the Zen Tricksters] started in 1979 as the Volunteers. The first ten years or so we just played in Long Island and New York City, sort of all in the tristate area, not much else. I can remember playing this movable Grateful Dead scene with this guy who would put on bands or dance parties all over the place, and we got hired to play a club on 42nd Street after a Madison Square Garden Dead show around '88 at a club called Jamming Room, a reggae club. The place was packed, and a guy came up to us and said, "Hey, I'm opening a bar downtown and I want you guys to play." We were like, "Yeah, yeah, okay"—you hear that kind of thing all the time. Well, come to find out it's Larry Bloch, and he was opening Wetlands. So we started playing there right from the get-go. I think we played there more than anyone else. That's the story I'm told.

Dean Budnick: I firmly believe in my heart of hearts that there would not be a Jambands.com, a Jammy Awards, or a modern-day *Relix* but for Larry Bloch and his efforts in founding Wetlands Preserve. Larry Bloch was an unabashed Deadhead, and when Wetlands opened in February 1989 the club served as a haven for a range of artists committed to improvisation in the live setting. New York is one of the most important media markets in the world, and Bloch's club became a beachhead for groups that otherwise could not find a place to perform in the city.

John Popper: I think from when Wetlands started and we kind of became the house band until the beginning of H.O.R.D.E. was really the time it felt to me like our scene. Again, that's my perspective of it, 'cause everywhere I looked it was Blues Traveler 'cause I was in the center of that. I think each band would probably have a story that is quite similar. I think to Mike Gordon it would be all about Phish—and then he bumped into the rest of the world.

Chris Barron: Well, Wetlands gave us a hard time—they took to Blues Traveler. We had to work really hard to get a gig there. This guy Walter booked the place, and on *Homebelly Grove,* our live record, he's the guy who is like, "Put your hand together for the Spin Doctors." I mean something like that. I knew Walter and I'd hang out there. Blues Traveler would be there, and I'd hang out with Blues Traveler, and it took us a long time to break into the Wetlands. It was a pain in the ass, but eventually we did and we were packing that place.

We called it the Manhattan tour. We just played. The thing is, back then, people went out more, and we didn't have as much competition from stuff at home. People had fun outside of their house instead of at home in front of the computer. If you wanted something cool to happen, you had to leave your house. If you wanted to, let's say, get some pussy, you had to leave your house. Now people can do computer sex or whatever. But back in the day you had to go find it for real. People went out a lot more. So we'd play every night, and people came. I think it was partly because we were doing weird stuff every night. Not one show was the same every night. So then guys like Kenny at the Bitter End was like, "You guys are the only band that can play every night, you and Blues Traveler—you're the only bands I know that can play every night and people would come out to see." I think it's because we were doing different stuff. We never knew what we were gonna play.

Well, I'll tell ya what happened—Blues Traveler got signed, they went on the road, then they weren't playing every night in New York. Then they were playing every month or every two months in New York. So then they got a huge show, and the same thing happened to us. We went out on the road and we were playing New

York every couple months. It was out of control, playing places like Roseland and places like that. It was just like mathematics—we weren't playing as much, so people were just coming out.

Jeff Mattson: Well, Wetlands was always a different place because it was made by hippies for hippies. They had the Eco Saloon with the area for the VW bus and flyers for all the causes and petitions you could sign, and they had meetings and were very serious about it. It was in the contract to keep that going. The owner wasn't going to sell if they didn't keep that going. Wetlands Preserve. There were always the drum circles downstairs and all kinds of crazy stuff, like they had speakers in the men's room and it sounded the best in there! It had a lot of character.

Dean Budnick: Another thing that really contributed to the mission of the club was the fact that although Larry had established it as a for-profit venture, it also supported a full-time environmental and social justice organization that was funded from $80 thousand to $100 thousand a year as an overhead expense. As Larry explains in the film [*Wetlands Preserved: The Story of An Activist Nightclub*, directed by Dean Budnick], "The idea was that the monetary cost of running an effective activism center wouldn't be impaired or tied into the profitability of the nightclub. It would be a necessary expense. Just like if we didn't pay the rent, we would be shut down. If we didn't fund the social and environmental activism center, we wouldn't be Wetlands."

There is no doubt in my mind that the good intentions that flowed from that commitment found their way into the general vibe of the club and on through the music.

A major part of Wetlands' legacy was that it became a proving ground and nurturing spot for emerging acts. People would come into the club on a weekend night based solely on the venue's reputation. They'd show up without even knowing the bands on the bill, just on faith because those groups had been selected to appear. That was quite extraordinary, and there are only a handful of music venues historically that have carried such clout. Of course this also meant that those groups had to attain a standard based not on their own reputations but rather on the reputation of the club itself. That could be a challenge, but those artists who thrived soon gained word-of-mouth, grassroots support and often a new measure of confidence as well.

Wetlands also became a means by which bands that had thrived in various regions of the country could come together and find like-minded players. In the film Dave Schools explains, "We always thought that Widespread Panic was the only band doing what we were doing until we came up here and we met Phish and eventually we met Blues Traveler and the whole H.O.R.D.E. scene started."

Alan Evans: Yeah, Wetlands was the spot you aspired to play. Back in the early Moon Boot Lover days we played little clubs like Kenny's Castaways and a bunch of little spots in the West Village, but then finally you get to Wetlands and that is like, "You made it." Especially back then, it was us, Screaming Headless Torsos, the Authority, Blues Traveler, God Street Wine, Spin Doctors, there were a ton.

Rob Derhak: We had to play so many crappy gigs in New York before we got a chance at Wetlands. For the jam band scene, the Wetlands was the heart of what there is now—and that built the scene. A lot of bands from New England and New York were feeding off that. Once those bands got big enough to move on, we just slid in with a few other bands into the Wetlands hole. It was all just filling by feeding off of each other.

Stephen Robinson: The first time we played at Wetlands I remember Jay [Bouman] was driving the band van into the city. I think we were coming from doing a show in Albany or a nearby college town the night before. At that time we generally tried to group our shows so we'd be out on the road for as little as a long weekend or as long as a few weeks at a time. We pulled into the side-street right next to Wetlands to load in. The load-in hallway was very narrow, and as it turned out, the band we were opening for, the Authority, had their equipment filling up the hallway. So we unloaded our equipment from the van and had it all in the alley waiting to bring it once the Authority moved their gear. At some point we heard a strange but loud noise from down the alley. It grew louder. Suddenly we saw what it was: a herd of rats charging down the street. They ran through, around, under, and over all our equipment! It was crazy and hilarious. Welcome to New York City and Wetlands!

Dean Budnick: The physical layout of the club was unlike any place I had ever encountered. The stage did not face out into the center of the room, and it was very low, all of which fostered a more intimate connection with the performers. Beyond that the lower level was filled with pillows and comfy chairs. It reminded me of my parents' paneled basement back in Rhode Island where we would hang out back in high school. It was that comfortable and familiar, all of which enriched the experience and made everything more friendly and personal.

Jeff Mattson: I think having a dedicated jam band place in New York City really meant something. It meant the rest of the country could look and say, "Well, they are recognizing it in New York City." All the bands that came to much greater fame came through there: Phish, Widespread Panic, Spin Doctors, Blues Traveler, all those bands, Warren Haynes, Joan Osborne, Dave Matthews. I saw the Donna Jean Godchaux Band there, and I became good friends with Donna. Now I've been playing with her for years.

Stephen Robinson: Once we got inside Wetlands we took a few minutes to look around and absorb the reality of playing in a venue with such history and significance. I remember reading all the band names that were signed in the back load-in hallway—everyone from huge New York City punk bands to grunge bands like Pearl Jam (who were, of course, enormously popular at that point) to all the fellow small-time bands that we knew and played with as we all crisscrossed our way around the East Coast college circuit. In those days, before YouTube and the Internet, I actually had no idea what the inside of Wetlands would look like before I played there. I remember thinking it was smaller than I expected and being surprised at the big pole right in the middle of the stage! We were used to playing venues of this size—mainly bars and event halls in the Northeastern college towns. We had also been opening for some of the bigger acts in those days, like Widespread Panic. In fact, Wetlands was not even in the top five biggest venues we had played from a strictly physical size perspective. But once I got on that stage, I felt like I was playing the most important gig of my life. I probably can't remember 99 percent of the gigs I played back in those days, just because of the time that has passed since then, but I definitely remember a number of moments from that show. We had a small group of fans that came just for us, although we were still pretty new to playing in New York City at that point. There were also a good number of Authority fans who had showed up early enough to give us a shot. I remember taking the time during our set to look at the other guys in the band and across the room and making sure I was taking it all in. When that crowd cheered, it sounded louder and more significant than cheers at other venues, regardless of whether it was actually louder. I also remember the Authority came on after us and showed us how the fuck it is done. That band was never given anywhere near their due. They blew the roof off every show we played with them over the years. They had women taking off their shirts. They had men dancing like giddy children. Their lead singer, Rene, just owned the stage. Hell, he owned the crowd! We left Wetlands desperately wanting to step up our game. We wanted to not just play there; we wanted to belong there. I'm sure a lot of bands felt that way—and in that sense I bet Wetlands helped improve the quality of live music in the jam scene far beyond the ways people traditionally think of. I think bands left there wanting to grow into the shoes that they had just had the honor of stepping into.

Dean Budnick: I'll always remember the first evening I was there past sunrise, which was a Blues Traveler show in 1990. They had to stop serving booze around 4 a.m., and they closed the rollgates out front so that it appeared to anyone driving past the venue that it was closed even as the band played on. It was quite extraordinary—those of us who were inside felt like we were part of a secret society, which, quite frankly, we were, drawn to a potent sound of thriving music outside the mainstream.

David Graham: Well, Arrowhead was our baby, actually, meaning me and my friend had a company called Music Unlimited, and at that point we did run those shows. When I speak of the inmates running the asylum, that might be one of the greatest examples of all time. It was a fly-by-night operation, but it was a lot of fun. I think it was of its time and slightly ahead of its time because it was needed, something that needed to be there. It sort of led into H.O.R.D.E., that concept, but what was great about that was it was before those bands really took off. None of them had really taken off yet, so it was like watching the heat rise off the desert. Not only did we have the jam band scene with Traveler, Phish, Spin Doctors, but we had the Band and people like Lenny Kravitz would come in. One night he played all night on the stage downstairs. Arrowhead was sort of a hippie complex, for lack of a better word. My dad died at the end '91, and we might have continued to do that had my life not completely changed, but it was a lot of fun.

Tom Constanten: Arrowhead was another magical venue to play at. You might remember that it wasn't that far physically from where the Woodstock festival was. Mostly what I remember about that was that Buddy Cage was along with the band. I was playing with a version of Gratefully Yours or Dead Ringers or whatever they called us at the time. He was seated to my right. As I was playing keyboard he launched into this marvelous solo, and I just stopped playing and watched. I didn't have a clue what he was doing. I have no idea how a pedal steel works. If you know Buddy, he has this angelic smile on his face and his good, overflowing, wonderful spirit that comes through with or without the music. The music just amplifies it.

Chris Barron: I'm not trying to say we invented that, but we definitely took a page out of the Acid Tests and all that kind of stuff. It was definitely inspired by all that. But nobody was doing it that we knew of. So I think Arrowhead was the apex of that, in a way. We went on and did the H.O.R.D.E. and stuff, so maybe H.O.R.D.E. was the apex of that whole thing. No, Arrowhead for sure was. There was something homemade about it. We just sort of found this ranch, "Oh, we are just like Woodstock! Like Yasgur's farm!" 'cause it's on a farm . . . it was just a great thing. Also there was a real sense of . . . what we were doing was taking off, a sense of walking and being like, "Oh my god, there is a lot of people here, a lot of people dig this." A lot of people came, more than had ever come before. It was also cool 'cause Phish was there. Blues Traveler and Spin Doctors—we had done gigs together, but I don't know how many gigs Phish, Blues Traveler, and Spin Doctors did together. It was the H.O.R.D.E. later on, but it was the H.O.R.D.E., that leg of H.O.R.D.E. dates, '92 I think it was. In the South we had Béla Fleck and the Flecktones. In the North we had Phish. I don't really know if we did five shows or if it was like fifteen. I don't really remember. But, yeah, it was definitely like a continuation of Arrowhead.

John Popper: Phish and Widespread—I think it was based on the fact that the Spin Doctors and us were largely Wetlands bands. But Wetlands drew Phish to it as it drew Widespread to it, so there was a connection there. But I think in our minds we met them out on the road. In my mind it was about touring with them. We had a gig with Widespread, someone would book us somewhere out on the road with them, and that's the thing—it kinda happened simultaneously. Once we started touring around 1990 outside of the city, then it was just a question of time before you ran into Phish fans and you started to see a Phish show. They also did come to New York, so you felt a bit like an ambassador.

Zach Newton: We were so young, it's hard to think of it. Now that I'm older I can look at the scene and assess, but back then it was just what it was. It wasn't a scene; it was just us doing our thing. J. B. and Mikey had a thing going; it was working and it felt really good. There wasn't a movement to make a jam band scene; it was just working toward that universal truth of doing what you love and were good at. That's what it was more than an intention to form a scene. We started to find each other. Phish, Blues Traveler—each band had a good following in their local area. It was like, "You should come up to the Northeast and open for us, and we'll come down and open for you." Popper, Blues Traveler—they were always the ones who wanted to push things bigger. They were the first to have a bus, the first to have a light guy, the first to think big. So Popper says, "Let's get all of us and do some shows and see if it works." That was probably the defining tipping point of "There is now an official jam band scene." It was the move to make something happen. Yeah, that was the first H.O.R.D.E. tour.

Béla Fleck: I don't remember how we ended up on the first H.O.R.D.E. tour, but it sure was fun. Let's see, Aquarium Rescue Unit, Blues Traveler, Spin Doctors, maybe Widespread Panic was on a couple of those. It was only four shows, and I don't think all the bands were on all the shows, but, boy, it was a lot of fun.

Col. Bruce Hampton [interview from *Swampland*]: Well, we'd been playing with Phish, Blues Traveler and Widespread Panic—everybody was there at the same time and nobody was doing much business. So John Popper asked me, "What would you guys do in the old days?" We toured with four or five bands to keep the ticket price down and do thirty- to forty-minute sets. That's how it was done. Especially in the R&B world, with six acts on one ticket . . . Aretha, B. B., Joe Tex, Solomon Burke, and Albert King for $2.50. That's how it worked back then. So, J. B., me, John, and Trey met in Bill Graham's office, and we wanted to keep the ticket prices down. We had six or seven groups on the bill . . . it was a phenomenal success.

It lasted seven or eight years. At the first of it we let all musicians run it and we didn't want to talk to ASCAP or floor drillers or whatever. Nobody wanted to deal with it or was capable of dealing with those small details. So it got turned over to people who could actually run the thing. It was a lot of fun. We had everybody in town sit in with us.

John Popper: We started H.O.R.D.E. The reason we took the forefront—there was two reasons—Bill Graham Presents was sort of gonna throw this and they were our managers, and also of all the bands, we had the most traveling. We'd been to the most places. Phish focused mostly on the Northeast, and Widespread focused on the Southeast, and Spin Doctors had a record that was doing great. The Aquarium Rescue Unit was tiny but everybody loved them. Then we had the range, and I was very aware of different scenes.

David Graham: I think John and I would probably have a fun time batting heads over where exactly H.O.R.D.E. came from. I think originally H.O.R.D.E. came from when John and I would go on the road and room together, and we spent a lot of time talking about the Dead. I would explain to him the kind of shows we did out west: camping shows. We had shows like where you would camp for three days and then, "Oh, by the way, it's time to go see the Grateful Dead." Walk out of your tent and go see the band. It was that kind of a spirit of a show—not necessarily camping overnight events, but sort of like that event experience that I think inspired John to come up with the idea, galvanizing this younger group of bands and taking them on the road, being more than just another show, which isn't easy. The first tour, I believe, it was Phish and Traveler . . . it was a pretty remarkable lineup considering where they all are now. I'm sure Dave Matthews did some H.O.R.D.E.s. I know the Crowes did a tour. I know the Allmans did a tour. I know Lenny played. It was a great array of music, and I think it came from the spirit of the Grateful Dead West Coast shows. Those shows were like the weekend destination where people would go, and it was relaxed and more than what was just on the stage. And in the case of H.O.R.D.E., whereas Lollapalooza had bells and whistles everywhere, it wasn't so much that H.O.R.D.E. did a bunch of other stuff; it was just the vibe, the feeling.

Parke Puterbaugh [from *Phish: The Biography*]: The scene that had been nurtured at Wetlands went national with the launching of H.O.R.D.E. The idea was to take a strength-in-numbers approach to help put the jam band scene on the map. The simple criteria, according to tour organizer John Popper of Blues Traveler: "Good bands that played well live." Popper, who was given to bold strokes, hailed from Anastasio's hometown of Princeton, as did Chris Barron of the Spin Doctors.

Dave Schools: The early H.O.R.D.E. tour was born out of necessity because here is a group of bands like Widespread Panic, Phish, Blues Traveler, Spin Doctors—Colonel Bruce Hampton and the Aquarium Rescue Unit and Béla Fleck and the Flecktones were also involved in the first one—we all developed strong regional followings and we all knew each other. We had played gigs with each other from the Georgia Theater and the Cotton Club down South to Ziggys in North Carolina, Iron Horse in Massachusetts, and, obviously, the Wetlands. We had all done that, but we couldn't get any one big national promoter to take a chance on us and help us move to arenas. Finally, out of necessity, we said, "Maybe if we all get together we can galvanize enough of our following to put ten to twelve thousand people in." So it was created out of necessity and was done with love. All the managers were kicked out of the original meeting, so the band members could plot and scheme, and it worked and it was fun and it felt like we were really blazing a new trail. And then, obviously, it took off. Most of the memories I have are the band segues where the Aquarium Rescue Unit would play and then we would wheel Blues Traveler up, and they would morph to a Blues Traveler set, and at the end of that we would wheel the Panic drums up, and there was a lot of cross-pollination. We all got to know each other, and maybe someday there will be a book about it and you probably shouldn't believe a word of it!

Dean Budnick: To see Aquarium Rescue Unit segue at the end of their set into Widespread Panic was quite unexpected and majestic. I had long viewed that segue as something of a bold political statement, asserting a one-for-all, all-for-one vibe that also extended to the audience as well. Then, twenty years later, when I interviewed John Bell for the *Relix* piece, he just laughed and corrected me, explaining that it was something slightly different: "It really started because we saw an extra fifteen minutes instead of doing the changeover. We saw the fifteen-minute window as an opportunity to do something different and continue to play and keep the music going. You really couldn't do it unless you had the larger stage and a bunch of young crew members willing to go, 'Whoa, okay, this is freaky, yeah, let's do it.' We wanted to stretch the usual parameters of normality in going to a concert. The other bands and managers were wondering what the crap was going on. 'Well you know, it's our time . . .'"

John Popper: I'll tell ya what happened—wanna hear the story? We are all in a meeting, all of Phish, all of Blues Traveler, and delegates from Widespread, Spin Doctors, Aquarium Rescue Unit, and, I think, Béla Fleck and the Flecktones. I told them my fantasy 'cause I was big into Attila the Hun and nomadic tribes pillaging, I was big into that. I'm part Hungarian, so, you know, that's a big thing with us. We pretend to be related to Attila the

Hun. Even though we're not. But still, we're similar. It's all in the perception. So someone suggests why don't we all just, no matter who is bigger in what area, just all equal billing, even money, nobody gets any more recognition, the littlest guy, the biggest guy, who cares? We actually sealed it in a jar of Vaseline that we had. This all in the office of Bill Graham in New York City. The very next day that very same person calls me and goes, "Sorry, we can't do that. Our manager says we need the money here!" So then I have to get on the phone and call that person that would hurt and then they go, "Okay, then we need the money here." On and on this goes, and I was the go-between for everybody. I think that's where it started, that I was in charge, is that because we traveled the most, we had relationships with the most bands, and I became the guy on the phone.

Stephen Perkins: We went to Reading Festival in England and . . . what a scene! We thought, why isn't this happening in America? We gotta make this happen! Lollapalooza started off like, "Who would you like to play at your party?" We had a list of twenty bands; we were only able to get five or eight of them, but that was really the idea—who would you want at your party? But it's great to see a package put together and especially if it's an eclectic package where you have a band doing one thing and then two hours later a band sounds completely different doing it and it's just as good and people are open to it. Then late at night there are these small little stages going all night. I'm a musician, and when I see all these different musicians there, I play better. At those festivals there are so many great players, and that to me is a benefit for the audience.

John Popper: The thing is, Lollapalooza in America started this idea that the European festivals did, and he wanted to take it on the road. It was Bill Graham working with Perry Farrell. Bill and Perry were doing that together, and that was the cool thing every year. The thing they did with the Grateful Dead, the New Years—it was that tradition of putting on a float and stuff that tripping people would look at and be like, "Holy shit, is that a giant caterpillar?" That met Perry Farrell's idea of a festival kind of thing. That's what started the summer tours.

Perry Farrell: Oh yeah, I, still to this day think he [Bill Graham] is the best promoter ever. I don't think he will ever be topped. It is hard these days—a lot has changed. This is my first time up here in and around Sausalito, and Alex Graham was telling me some stories like how his mom met his dad—her being a waitress, and his dad came into the restaurant too drunk to drive and asked her to drive him home and that's how it began. Those were ripe times to experiment and enjoy as a youngster.

Stephen Perkins: There is some history with Bill Graham and Jane's Addiction. We actually tried to do a Jane's Addiction/Grateful Dead show at The Coliseum in Los Angeles. They sold about seventy-eight thousand tickets, and Bill called us and said if you can sell the next fifteen, we could make it over one hundred thousand, but it didn't work out 'cause of a few different things. We were traveling and tried to come back to do it. I did make it to the show, but the other guys were still out of town. It turned out they had a small riot on the floor, and I know if Jane's played, we would have been blamed for it, so I'm happy we didn't play! That was in '90, I believe, because we started doing Bill shows at Cal Expo and the Fillmore and even the Warfield when Jane's first started. He showed us a good time and how to put on a show. No one promoted a show like him. You get backstage and you feel like you're in a fantasy world with the Bill Graham show.

David Graham: I remember a time my dad and I were walking around in Paris and listening to our Walkmans and we were listening to Blues Traveler, and we were both sort of dancing. So I knew then that he liked them.

Perry Farrell [**from *Whores***]: Marc Geiger [William Morris booking agent; conceptualized and cofounded Lollapalooza with Perry Farrell] encouraged me to be creative. He said, "Do whatever you want on this summer tour. Get whoever you want to open for you." I just went to him with this wish list of groups that I liked . . . and came up with a name . . . I think I got it thumbing through the dictionary. Lollapalooza is someone or something very striking or exceptional, number one. And number two, it's a giant swirling lollipop.

David Graham: H.O.R.D.E. and Lollapalooza are very much alike. When Lollapalooza first came around, it was in '91. Perry asked for $30,000 from every local promoter to do the concourse stuff. I think they all said no except at the last show, which was Shoreline, and my dad said sure. That was where Lollapalooza was born, the one we all know, the Lollapalooza with the Jim Rose Circus, with the freaks, with the fire, that started at a BGP [Bill Graham Presents] show when Dad acquiesced to Perry and set him off. So it was there I think people really saw it was more than just some progressive bands playing. That is what we tried to do with H.O.R.D.E.—more of the nonmusical stuff on the stage.

Perry Farrell: The fellow who is most responsible for Lollapalooza celebrating the twentieth anniversary was Bill Graham. The reason is because when I did it that first year Bill was one of the promoters. Of course in those days there were many promoters. Promotion was regional—if you go to Cincinnati there was a different guy, if you go to Washington Seth Hurwitz, you go to San Francisco and it was Bill Graham—so every Lollapalooza was a little different because you are under the sway of that promoter and what he would do for that particular show. Some promoters did nothing; you would be lucky if you got ice. When you went to San Francisco you were greeted by topless women with their boobs painted and a drum circle going on. Bill Graham made Lollapalooza come to life. I spoke with him, and he said I was doing a really good thing. He died shortly after; it might have been the next year, unfortunately. Immediately the picture came to life of what this festival could be, and everybody was inspired to repeat it and do it again. I met the brother of David [Graham] that year, Alex, who is now one of my best friends.

John Popper: We said, well, why not a hippie version? We wanted to call it Lollapatchouli. But we wanted people to take it seriously, and my fantasy, being into Attila the Hun, was: it's a cold day someplace in Kansas when, in from the south, comes Widespread Panic fans consuming everything in their way, and from the north are Phish fans, and from the east come Blues Traveler, and from the west comes Béla Fleck. Of course, that never happens—everyone is coming from a different direction. I was being very naïve here, but I saw a torrent of convergence of different audiences, and that was my fantasy.

Dean Budnick: [from *Relix* magazine]: After [Mike] Gordon returned home from the initial meeting, he drew up an extended list that he circulated via fax. The options also included the Farm-Fresh Banana Festival, the Sir James Isaac Newton Summer Jam, East Coast Diner Poached Egg Music Fest, Seven Hours of Noise, Saltwater Taffy Twisting Machine Festival, Marshmellow Music, Five Bands That Stink, Summer Glacier Meltdown, and Big Big

Spinach Rock Party. One last-minute addition was the Clifford Ball. The name appears with an asterisk and a note on top that explains, "Clifford Ball's name was on a plaque in the airport. We saw the plaque while finding a phone to call John Popper. 'A Beacon of light in the world of flight.' We can get more info on this guy and recreate his world."

Widespread Panic circulated its own list that included such names as Deli Tray, Trust Fund Hobo Fest, Cavalcade of the Large, Corn Dodgers, and Summer of Flesh. The group also threw its support behind some of the Phish suggestions as well as ARU's We Aren't the World before concluding, "Widespread Panic does it like the Great American H.O.R.D.E., without shame." Still, there was something so special about the Clifford Ball that Phish manager John Paluska sent one final fax making a case for the name with an accompanying piece of artwork created by Jim Pollock.

John Popper: It was like a H.O.R.D.E., so I wanted an anagram that spelled "H.O.R.D.E.." It was Horizons of Rock Developing East Coast, 'cause all these bands were from the East Coast. Eric Schenkman said, no, it should be everywhere, that way we can get anybody. And he was exactly right. So that's what it became. It was just a way to have all these bands and not be in the clubs in the summer. That was all we wanted.

That first year we lost about eight grand, and it looked like an emaciated third-world ghetto. There was like coyotes eating out of tin cans and a really thin hippie with just his hand out. It was brutal. Then the second year the Allman Brothers got involved. The first year Jones Beach was great, and there was a Northern leg with Phish and a Southern leg with Widespread; each one had a really good one and really crappy one and two okay ones. I made each band a sword that each of us has! I saw Widespread's on Facebook. Of course with me it had to be a real sword. I don't play around—what's the point of a fake sword? Phish got theirs first. It was a full thirty-five-inch broadsword, full-bladed, sharper than the devil himself, with a handle of a green hand holding an orb and on it was "molta et valuta modulate et vincite," which means, rock-and-roll jam and conquer. It had every band's logo on it as the first congregation of the great American horde. We took Phish's and put a peach on a bucket on top of a road case and Trey swung at it. It went through the peach, through the pit, into the bucket and straight through the road case. We just wanted to see if it worked.

Dave Schools: It is still up in our office! The H.O.R.D.E. sword was a great gift from John, a giant medieval battle axe with the names and logos of all the bands on the first H.O.R.D.E. tours etched into the blade.

Parke Puterbaugh [from *Phish: The Biography*]: The funny thing was, even when Phish were ostensibly part of a movement like H.O.R.D.E., in reality they were only tangentially connected. As if to separate themselves from the pack, Anastasio and Mc-Connell later pointed out that Phish appeared only on the first four shows of the first H.O.R.D.E. tour. H.O.R.D.E. continued to package jam bands for years after that, but Phish was never again among them. While they supported the all-for-one concept and benefited from the national exposure H.O.R.D.E. received, they were obviously an entity unto themselves who were meant to go it alone. Nonetheless, back in the States among the kindred spirits of H.O.R.D.E., they hammered it up at Jones Beach Amphitheater on Long Island. The group wore masks while singing their barber-shop quartet opener ("Sweet Adeline") and let Fishman rip on the vacuum cleaner toward the end.

David Graham: I think he [Bill Graham] was just taken with the music. I think he didn't have too much tolerance for the fly-by-night aspect of it. He had to come in and lay down the law a few times. He would say, "When you are in the band, that is when you can stay up until four in the morning!" But when you're not in the band, and a lot of us weren't, it doesn't work. But we all wanted to have a good time! He wasn't thrilled with the business acumen of everybody, but he certainly loved the music. He dug Blues Traveler a lot, and we were closest with them because we managed them, but he liked all of them. There was also a time when I think, for him, in the sixties and seventies, he made bands play together a lot, especially at the Fillmore, which is why it's famous. You had the Dead with Miles Davis, you had an incredible confluence of musicians, and in the seventies he was able to do that on a bigger level, like Days on the Green in California, where it wouldn't be one headliner—it would be, like, five bands. My favorite story is at Days on the Green where Aerosmith headlined and Ted Nugent was second, or Van Halen opened and AC/DC was the second band. Well, the eighties came along, and it sort of became more of "We are U2, here is our show." It wasn't quite the same. When this scene came around and you see all them playing together, and he saw what happened with H.O.R.D.E. and Lollapalooza, sort of like a coming together of the bands, he really enjoyed that. And this scene was really all about that. Plus, these were all friends and you could tell—everyone felt connected to it, they felt invested, and that makes a big difference, and he clearly was into that.

Dean Budnick: I was at that first H.O.R.D.E. show at the Cumberland County Civic Center in Portland, Maine, on July 9, 1992, and it was a revelation. I had grown up in New England, so I had been enjoying the music of Phish for a few years at that point. I had seen Blues Traveler, Widespread Panic, and Spin Doctors in

New York City at Wetlands, but the club only held a few hundred people (the legal capacity was 389, but Larry Bloch felt the "true" capacity was a few hundred more). Never did I imagine that these bands could fill a hockey arena or an amphitheater nor did I think that Col. Bruce Hampton and Aquarium Rescue Unit, the only band on the bill that I hadn't yet seen, would be the special sauce to make it happen.

The walk to the venue from my car was a thrill. It soon became evident that plenty of folks were just as interested in this collection of bands as I was. Many had driven in from out of state like myself and were standing outside their vehicles playing the music that had brought them. As I wrote in a *Relix* piece commemorating the twentieth anniversary of that inaugural tour, "It was like the boosterish of the 1920s all over again, but rather than preaching the virtues of their local townships, the focus was on music borders or perhaps the lack thereof, given the range of improvisation reflected in that quilt of sound."

Stepping inside was another shock to the system in the best way possible. There were thousands of people quite literally showing their colors, decked out in tie-dyes and more commonly in the T-shirts of their favorite bands. Even though none of the groups were getting much in the way of mainstream coverage at that time, everyone had somehow been exposed to their music, and like me, they had caught the bug. Again, this is before the Internet carried much resonance, so I had no idea what to expect nor was I in communication with many like-minded music fans outside my immediate circle of friends, but here we all were. It was a glorious thing.

The Great American H.O.R.D.E.: *Relix* Review of the first H.O.R.D.E. Tour: Comprised of five bands, H.O.R.D.E. was perhaps rock 'n' roll's most notable achievement of the summer of 1992. H.O.R.D.E. is an acronym for Horizon of Rock Developed

Everywhere [sic], and took the form of a new music festival which
traveled throughout the east coast in July and August.

The northeast migration of the Great American H.O.R.D.E.—
Col. Bruce Hampton and the Aquarium Rescue Unit, Blues Traveler, Phish, Spin Doctors, and Widespread Panic—made tracks from
Portland, Maine, across much of New York, and included a memorable detour in New Jersey. Playing for a total of approximately
25,000 fans, the H.O.R.D.E.—pioneering young bands, each with
its own unique perspective—united under a colorful banner with
the common premise of exploring the boundaries of rock.

Each H.O.R.D.E. show consisted of over six hours of live
music, almost uninterrupted as a result of logistical wonders performed by an extended and efficient stage crew and production
team. The bands received equal billing and equal time, each playing roughly an hour and fifteen minutes. At successive gigs on the
tour, each band's performance varied enough to further reveal to
the audiences just how much musical prowess was lurking in the
summer air. H.O.R.D.E. subverted regional limitations by bringing the southern twirls of the ARU and Widespread Panic to upstate New York, and the gritty, upbeat groove of the Spin Doctors
to Birmingham, Alabama.

The Aquarium Rescue Unit of Atlanta, Georgia opened all
of the northeast dates, an appropriate situation considering their
masterful improvisation and their attitude toward song structure.

Col. Bruce Hampton explained, "Our idea was to take every
kind of music that had purity left (bluegrass, jazz, and blues) and
let it go. We never rehearse, and while we have a format, I'm not
sure what it is."

ARU drummer Apt. Q258 added, "In all the six or so years that
I've been playing with Col. Bruce we've rehearsed twice. Some
tunes have a definite structure which we stick to, but usually
it's free and open enough that if anyone in the band wants to do

something as strange as vomit in the middle of a jam we could all respond accordingly."

From Athens, Georgia came Widespread Panic, a psychedelic confederacy with no qualms about stepping into the Aquarium Rescue Unit's southern-tipped, improvising shoes. Literally. One by one, the members of Widespread Panic came out on stage and started jamming as the ARU was finishing its set, eventually replacing the ARU with Widespread Panic. Add John Popper from Blues Traveler on harmonica and the essence of H.O.R.D.E. takes center stage: musicians who have similar enough outlooks to actually pull off live, whole band segues without disturbing the pelvic swinging of thousands of delighted fans.

Widespread Panic spontaneously combusted in nearly every song, taking jams so far out on a limb that if one was to stop and think about how to categorize their music, the best part of the show would most likely have been missed—musical traditions which are deconstructed and recombined in ways that often defy categorization, a fresh musical state for the nineties.

Bassist David Schools of Widespread Panic said, "Beyond any musical similarities, the H.O.R.D.E. bands have a common spirit." Keep this in mind and imagine the transition from almost two and a half hours of southern-tinged, breathy jams to the unquestionably urban Spin Doctors. Where the Doctors are concerned, lyrical content carries more of the message and the screw of song structure is tightened just a bit. A Spin Doctors jam is like looking through a microscope, as compared to the more telescopic jamming of the Aquarium Rescue Unit and Phish. The Doctors may cover a little less ground in terms of improvisation, but the trade-off is that they can explore it with exacting detail. At Jones Beach, under gleaming emerald lights, the Doctors took the audience on an extended trip in "What Time Is It," inducing a lengthy guitar-soaked jam with a concretely funky beat.

Chris Baron, singer and songwriter for the Spin Doctors, characterized the H.O.R.D.E.: "All the bands are above a certain level of quality . . . really good bands . . . with an ethic of jamming. H.O.R.D.E. gave us all a chance to play some big, important venues."

Gigs at notable venues are synonymous with the exponential increase in the success and notoriety of the H.O.R.D.E. bands in the last year. During the year, the Doctors toured hard and well, bringing the beat and the word to thousands across the nation. As the weather warmed, so did the mainstream aesthetic. In the first two months of summer, the Doctors appeared on "Late Night with David Letterman" and "The Dennis Miller Show," as well as performing at New York City's legendary Long Star, a gig sponsored by radio station WNEW.

"Music and popular movements operate on geometric curves, rather than straight lines," Baron said. "Once word of mouth reaches a certain point, the numbers take astronomical leaps. What people want suddenly comes to be available."

Unfortunately, one thing that wasn't available was a completely democratic environment for two of the H.O.R.D.E. shows—the July 11th gig at the Garden State Performing Arts Center in New Jersey, and the July 12th gig at the Jones Beach Theater. One of the things about the H.O.R.D.E. tour that made it so notable was the animated, informative and diverse concourse of vending and awareness which traveled with the tour. Concert-goers could wade through environmental and political displays, as well as a small carnival of vendors. Controversy arose when governmental regulations prevented three groups—NORML (National Organization for the Reform of Marijuana Laws), NOW (National Organization for Women), and Planned Parenthood—from participating in the concourse.

Tempers flared as First Amendment rights seemed to be violated. Both Chris Baron and John Popper expressed—onstage and off—their concern over this issue.

"The responsibility I hold," said Baron in an interview, "is the burden of liberty. Theoretically, I'm allowed to say what I want and I'm allowed to distribute the information that I want. Maybe what bands should try and do is to raise everyone to that level of responsibility. The same people that empower us [the bands], empower themselves."

"We really encouraged every group with a grievance and [a] table to come down to the shows," said Popper. "We're trying to stimulate people's thinking; it's an election year and we want to encourage people to vote."

Laying down tune after tune, Blue Traveler's melodies snaked all over the jumping and popping rhythms, inevitably diving head first into a huge gonzo jam replete with screaming guitar solos and frantic harmonica runs. The boys jam to a certain intensity and then maintain it steadily, driving the crowd into a frenzy. At the head of the frenzy, encouraging the crowd to beckon the moon out of the clouds, wearing an ominous, black bird-like mask and strumming an acoustic guitar was John Popper.

At their Jones Beach, New York performance Phish responded to the seaside location and the audience's willingness with expansive versions of "Divided Sky" and "Fluffhead," as well as newer jam tunes like "Maze." As the closing act on the H.O.R.D.E. tour, Phish continuously revitalized the crowd with their distinctive world of organic jamming, a musical arrangement where the sum of the parts and the whole are one in the same.

The band's high order of live performance comes from a rigorous rehearsal schedule (sandwiched in between an even more rigorous tour schedule), and a dedication to communication, on and offstage. Trey Anastasio (guitarist, singer, songwriter) likens playing with Phish to, "a musical conversation, where one person is playing a phrase, and I'm thinking in contrary terms. I try to come up with something spontaneously that answers against that phrase."

Instrumental in H.O.R.D.E.'s conception, execution and success was Blues Traveler. Members of the Traveler family were involved in many levels of H.O.R.D.E.'s production for months before the actual events, although it is John Popper who is credited with engineering the tour.

"He put months of work into it . . . really hard work . . . putting up with a lot of bullshit, all the bands' demands and whatever," Baron said. Popper's sense of responsibility to the community, fostered in large part by the activities of his band, is admirable. He was an unusually visible presence, leading several parades and processionals in and around the various venues.

Traveler guitarist Chan Kinchla continued, "We realized that in addition to the music, there's a lot of people out there doing very interesting things that we're hip to. We want to give them as much of a chance to express themselves as we have. One thing music can do is bring a lot of people together."

What Are Jam Bands and Where Did They Come From?

Horace Moore [interview from *Bands That Jam*]: Yeah, it was kind of interesting because it originated, in a sense, as a one-by-one deal. The first time I ever saw JB perform Dave and I actually went and saw him together after a Georgia Bulldogs football game. It was on a Saturday afternoon in early October of '84, I believe. We had heard about this guy that played a lot of different kinds of music—Dead tunes and stuff. He was playing down at this bar after the game. We went and checked him out and had a blast. It was a lot of fun.

A few weeks later, by a chance meeting with a mutual friend of his that became our friend, we ended up meeting JB. He and Dave met; JB already knew Mikey. I saw JB and Mikey play, and before you know it, Dave's beginning to play the bass with them. So the first time I see those three together is, literally, in a living room, over on King Avenue, here in Athens. Then they started playing some parties and stuff.

It was a good year after that when Todd finally showed up and they called it an official band, with a regular drummer. February 6,

1986 at the Mad Hatter Ballroom, here in Athens. That was their first gig, but long before then, a lot of friends just hanging around. It's just like any other college scene where some people are playing music. This was one of those things that just had a real special spark to it. It just kind of grew from there. It was a real friendly, hangout, community scene there at the very beginning. I think everybody played the bongos and served as the drummer at one time, hanging out at the house. It was one of those things that just grew from friends into something that grew into something else.

John Bell [interview from *Georgia* magazine]: The band house—that's where the earliest memories came from and where daydreaming and living in the moment didn't necessarily cancel each other out.

We were (at the time) four guys living on King Avenue with a kitchen full of band gear and a lot of time on our hands. At one point in the day we'd wake up, go into town for food and adventure (sometimes work). Then we'd find each other again—most likely at the Uptown Lounge or back at the house.

We put on our latest scratchy albums—I remember Warren Zevon and R.E.M. being the most resistant to damage. If someone had an inspiration, we'd make our way to the kitchen, play off each other, and see what would come of it. A lot of kidding around, a lot of beer.

Friends would stop by on a whim. If there was enough whimsy in the air at night, all of a sudden we'd be hosting a party. I don't think we ever planned a party, because so many spontaneous gatherings erupted. Fun for us, but we lived next door to a city councilman, so Athens's finest routinely and politely stopped by for a visit as well. We could ask ten to twenty people to lower the overall volume, but if there were more, we'd usually have to shut our doors and turn the lights off for the night.

Returning home after one of our first road trips—probably to Clemson, Greenville, and Charlotte—our next-door neighbors on the other side commented on how much our playing had improved. They didn't know we had been out of town, letting another Athens band, the Landsharks, use the house for practice.

Kyle and Duck at the Uptown introduced us to Sunny and gave us our first piece of rock 'n' roll security—a regular Monday night gig for what came through the door: $1 cover. That was a big deal. Playing a whole night in front of people was a lot different than being back at the house. Our first show was over, and we still owed the bar for our drink tab. Mike's sister bailed us out on that. Later Kyle said draft beer could be part of the deal. We were honing our negotiation skills.

Early one summer UGA was in between sessions, and the town was empty of students. It was lucky for us, though, because with the kids gone, the locals came out, and we were maybe the only game in town. About three hundred–plus folks came through. Widespread Panic was on its way . . . to Waffle House. "The Girls House" had us over for dinner on Sundays. Chicken wings. These were good friends that lived together on Buena Vista Street and looked after us. Mondays we ate yellow food (Waffle House). The rest of the week was ramen noodles, apples, hot dogs and an occasional pizza. Candles replaced electricity, blankets replaced gas, and the landlords were mostly patient. We were having a blast.

Zach Newton: We were so small that frat gigs were welcome. Everyone was playing frat houses—that was the money gig. The 40 Watt, but that was more of the early grunge band than the jam scene. It was small town and intermingling. But I would definitely say the Uptown Lounge, which was the birthplace of Panic, and the Georgia Theater. I worked house sound, local sound, Georgia Theater, before proceeding to the Uptown Lounge.

Horace Moore [interview from _Bands That Jam_]: I kind of
got introduced to the Dead by a dude named Tom Merrill who
lived out in Colorado. He gravitated toward the taper thing immediately. We'd grown up together as well. He introduced me to that
whole thing, and it just took off. That really segued into how I met
Dave Schools. His first day of school at Georgia in the fall of '83,
a friend of mine who was living in the dorm across the hall from
him, he realized that Dave had a lot of Grateful Dead tapes, called
me up, and said, "Dude, you have to come over here and meet this
guy." So that was it. The whole magnetism of the taping experience really pulled me into that whole thing. It really opened up a
lot of friendships, experiences, and opportunities for me down the
road. It was destined, I guess, in a certain way.

Dave Schools: Panic got together, and we didn't know how to
play; we learned how to play together as a group. All of us liked the
Grateful Dead except for Mike Houser, who didn't dislike them;
they just weren't on his radar. He grew up near Chattanooga and
was listening to a lot of southern rock. He loved Black Sabbath.
His favorite guitar player was Steve Howe of Yes. So he got the
mind-trip part of the music. So we learned how to play together and created an ensemble. None of us were especially terrific
musicians as individuals, but we created a language, and I think
that is what we learned from the Grateful Dead—that it's the ensemble that matters, and it's what you say when you're performing
together onstage, the ability to listen and hear each other and have
a musical conversation. If there is one gift that the Grateful Dead
gave to the future bands of the world it's this: this is some important stuff—it's not just playing things correctly, it's not just creating
this big two dimensional performance—it's this thing that occurs,
it's participatory, and, by virtue of being participatory, it engulfs
the audience and they become participants too and then it goes

to the next level, and that's a really important thing. It's crept into other music, this spirit. I think it's something the jazz players have understood for a while and possibly even real blues players. It has this participatory nature, and it's a big benchmark. It's the most important aspect of the whole thing.

Zach Newton: I don't ever want to qualify them as a Dead cover band. It was a smaller thing back then. That's what it was coming out of. Some of what they brought to the scene was they were a little bit older. JB and Mikey were a little bit older than the rest of the early H.O.R.D.E. bands. So they were bringing stuff in like the Talking Heads, some of that "kill your television" type. They had other stuff we didn't know about. We were all discovering how many different musics there were at the time. Mikey had the Black Sabbath stuff and taught us it wasn't just loud grungy rock. It was "listen and see what I'm getting from this." As far as what was the spark, for me, through all of this—it's been the ones who succeeded. It was coming from a place of honesty and love and back to doing what you want to do and doing it really well and being lucky enough that everything lined up, time-wise and music-wise. The Dead got people into the jammy thing. The people were old enough, and they were drawing from different musics. Palusca, Phish's old manager, has one of the most incredible jazz collections I've ever seen. So that poured, and of course Bruce [Col. Bruce Hampton] was the ultimate—knew everything about music.

With Bruce, going way back, well, my best friend in kindergarten was Tarman Kelly. Tarman's dad was the lead guitar player for the Hampton Grease Band, which was pretty active back in the late sixties in the Southeast. It was a jam band scene back then. It was just one or two bands doing it. So I used to go to Tarman's house, and that is where they rehearsed. Then I went up to Athens for school and saw Bruce's name, so I walked in. Childhood memory thing—I walked in and he was onstage playing. He pointed to the back of the room, right at me, "You, you—you're the kid with the big head," he says. His knowledge, his . . . more . . . awareness—there's a lot of stuff, a lot of generality that he throws out that tend to be universal truths and seem like he's seeing something psychic, but it's more knowledge of how the world works.

Jimmy Herring [interview from *Digital Interviews*]: I was lucky enough to meet some of the most incredible players in town, and they all introduced me to Col. Bruce Hampton—and it was over! He gave us a lesson in life that we could have never gotten from any school anywhere.

We got a taste of what real freedom was. He used to say all the time, "Freedom can be a prison." He was right. That kind of freedom can be a prison if you don't know how to handle it. The kind of music that we were playing [in Aquarium Rescue Unit] was a lot like Dead music. It could be different every night. You were free to do anything you wanted to do. If you wanted to come on stage with one string on your guitar and "do-ing-do-ing-do-ing" on one string all night, that was fine as long as you really meant it.

Oh yeah, it was great, because I've never really fit into any one style. I couldn't play rock 'n' roll legitimately because I was too influenced by jazz. I couldn't play jazz legitimately because I was too influenced by rock 'n' roll. I was in a country band for about seven months, and that almost killed me! Not because of the music as much as the guys I was playing with—it was a "Top Forty" thing. But it was a good learning experience, and I wouldn't trade it for anything. I couldn't play any of those things legitimately because I was so influenced by all of them. To me it was all the same thing—music. I thought that was going to be a problem until I played with Bruce, because that's what he wanted to do. He called it American Roots Music. It was bluegrass, blues, funk, and jazz. Those were the four primary elements. We had this mandolin player, this guy was as good as anybody. Matt Mundy—he's probably the greatest bluegrass mandolin player ever.

Col. Bruce Hampton [interview from *Swampland*]: They [Widespread Panic] are probably the nicest band I ever met at the time. Always have been. They were so young when they started. They used to work and play at the Uptown Lounge in Athens. Dave was the doorman, Todd tended bar, and I think JB was hanging around playing the pinball machines. I remember thinking about Dave Schools at the time, "Wow, this young guy really knows a lot about music. More than anyone I've ever heard." He was discussing Miles, Trane, and Monk. I was just blown away by his musicality. Panic was a breath of fresh air. In the eighties everyone had bad hair and stupid shoes. They were good cats. They were at the right place at the right time, and it worked. You just didn't find people like them. There weren't people like that back then. It was really positive and uplifting to see people with such good intentions.

Béla Fleck: One of the things I remember about Colonel Bruce is that he could walk up to someone, look them in their eyes, and tell their birthday. He would do it over and over again and only once in a while miss it, but not often. That was one of those things that made people believe he had spiritual powers. A really neat guy.

Zach Newton: His ability, I don't know if anyone has gotten this, his birthday-guessing ability. That was another one. Again, I was living in Athens and briefly saw him. Then I was hanging out with the Widespread Panic guys at the time in the early jam band scene. We all worked at the same bar they played every Monday night—they played Dead covers every Monday night, that's how Panic started—and we ended up in a hotel with Bruce one night. He was like, "Your birthday is February 24th, and you're my sound engineer." I had not really ever run sound before, and two weeks later I was standing in a two thousand–seat auditorium opening for Phish, looking for the on-off switch. By the end of the night I was proficient at it.

Col. Bruce Hampton [interview from *Swampland*]: To me, music has to come from the church, folk music, or outer space. You can be a sophisticated folk singer, but it's got to come from those places or I can't listen to it. Or it doesn't make sense to me. It's gotta have a story and some soul. I want to hear from the people who have nothing to say instead of those who want to say something. . . . The number-one thing to learn in life is to get rid of EGO, which stands for Edging God Out. When you think you're doing something, you're in bad trouble. There's a thing called faith and there's a thing called confidence, and then there's a nasty thing called ego. That's a tricky thing. You can't let ego cripple you. I've seen it ruin people more than drugs, booze, or relationships. That's what usually kills a band or a football team or whatever—ego. For others, it's drinking, drugs, and relationships. Clarity is also a danger for me.

Jimmy Herring [interview from *Guitar World*]: The Aquarium Rescue Unit and Phish used to play together quite a bit back in the old days. We were coming up at the same time, and you knew those guys were going to be huge. They were really cool to us. We would go up to the northeast and open for Phish, and then they would come down south and open for us in places like Atlanta and Tuscaloosa. And we would be laughing like, "Phish is opening for us—what a joke!" because we knew they were going to take over the world. You could see it coming, and eventually they did.

Trey Anastasio [interview from *Gadiel.com*]: We met in Vermont. Three of us graduated from Goddard College, an alternative school from the sixties, where you design your own course of study. For example, I worked with a composer, Ernie Stires, who taught me arranging for three years. I wrote a couple of musicals, big-band arrangements, atonal pieces. Meanwhile, Fish was locked in a room with a drum set for three years.

Trey Anastasio [from *The Phish Book*]: After the ROTC dance we played in '83, our second gig was a free show in the basement of the University of Vermont's Slade Hall. It said a lot about the direction the band would eventually take. We wanted to play original tunes right off the bat, and we also wanted our own light show. So one of Mike's earliest projects was a huge plywood box with switches on it that operated a rack of colored lights that hardly lit anything. We dragged in a huge curving geometric plane for a backdrop, then collected our various stereo speakers and hung them from the ceiling facing different directions. I was a DJ at WRUV at the time, and another DJ, our friend Anne Labruciano, mixed sound effects on six turntables while we played. It took us all day to load all this junk into Slade, and we played for about twenty people.

Parke Puterbaugh [from *Phish: The Biography*]: On December 1, 1984, Phish ascended a rung on the local club scene by playing their first gig at Nectar's. This combination restaurant, bar, and music venue on Main Street in downtown Burlington, with its familiar revolving sign over the sidewalk, has long been a local institution. The operation was owned by Nectar Rorris, a

Greek entrepreneur with a soft spot for music. . . . At first Phish performed not on Nectar's main stage but at the less prestigious upstairs room (which is currently Metronome Club). . . . Hunt's, a cool club that presented music most nights of the week, also played a critical role as a live venue for Phish in their developmental years. . . . By fall of 1986 they were playing well-attended gigs at Hunt's and getting to play downstairs at Nectar's too. . . . From November 1986 through March 1989 they had an informal residency at Nectar's, performing every month or two on some combination of Sunday, Monday, and Tuesday nights. Their increasingly loyal fans would show up every time they were booked, even if it was a three-night stand.

Chris Kuroda [from *Phish: The Biography*]: My experience of Phish at Nectar's was that I couldn't leave and I couldn't stay away. And that was a very common thing. Many times I said, "One set and I'm going home," and it never happened. It was addicting. *Unbelievably* addicting.

Amy Skelton [from *Phish: The Biography*]: It was kind of like a Phish show [in the later years], where you had serious hippies who were doing the whole tour and sleeping in their cars, and then you had kids coming out who were pretty clean cut and did well in school and obviously came from money. You had that same thing going on even at the Nectar's stage of the game.

John Fishman [from *Phish: The Biography*]: For five years we had Nectar's and other places around town to play from nine until two in the morning. We'd get three-night stands, so we didn't even have to move our equipment. Basically, the crowd was our guinea pig. We'd have up to five hours to do whatever the hell we wanted.

Trey Anastasio [from *Phish: The Biography*]: We really took things out at Nectar's. We did the play [*Gamehendge*] there, and we did a lot of songs where people would come onstage and do weird things . . . There wouldn't be a Phish without Nectar's.

Trey Anastasio [interview from *High Times*]: If you kind of followed the Phish path, if you're into Phish, we always used to talk about all these weird exercises we would do. First, we used to play for eight hours, all night, drink marijuana hot chocolate and eat mushrooms, and then we would do listening exercises, and then we would do improvisations on one note.

Trey Anastasio [interview from *The Believer*]: We had this series of exercises we developed called, "Including Your Own Hey." It sounds weird, but we did them a lot. They start off with a pulse. The first level is, I play a four-note phrase. Page is on my right, and he imitates it on the piano. Fish does his best to play it on the drums, then Mike does it on the bass. Now everyone goes around the room in a circle and everyone starts one.

Yeah, and then there were more levels. The next level is, I start with a pattern and then Page harmonizes with it. We make a jigsaw puzzle pattern. Then Mike finds his place in the pattern, and Fish finds his place in it. And we're all listening to each other. Now, only when you hear that all the other musicians have stopped searching, once you hear they've locked in with what you're play- ing, you say, "Hey!" So since we're still listening so intently to each other, we should all say, "Hey" at the same time, but if we don't, if someone says, "Hey" when you're still searching, they've basically just told you, "I'm not listening to you." So we found, very quickly, that it meant you had to always be listening to three people other than yourself. And the music, we found, improved immensely by not navel gazing. So now the idea is, I'm not paying any attention to myself at all. I'm just responding to what they're playing.

John Rider: My first memory of Mike [Gordon] was when he came up to me with sheet music in one hand and a cassette in another. He said, "I have a recording of you doing 'Emotional Railroad' and I transcribed your guitar solo." And there was "Emotional Railroad" on one channel and me playing bass on the other channel.

Mark Mercier: One of my first memories was when they, the whole band [Phish], came to the Living Room one night and sat down with us in the dressing room. They were going around to different bands and picking their brains—how they got there and what they did. It was almost like we were being interviewed by them. As a matter of fact, later on we sat down and said, "They picked our brains; we should pick theirs." We told Scott to go call Mike Gordon. All of a sudden there was a meeting of the minds with Scott and Mike, and they sat down and developed a relationship.

Trey Anastasio [interview from *High Times*]: I was very, very into the Dead in 1982–83, which was right when Phish started. Then I kind of got into Phish. When you're in your own band, that becomes the focus of your life. But I always loved them, and I didn't get to see them as much as I had in that period. I don't think I saw a Dead show for seven years. I saw them in San Francisco in '94 or '95. It was definitely an eye opener. Having not seen it and coming back to it, it was a little bit shocking how much things had changed. . . . I love the Dead. I always thought that anybody who thought that they could be replaced by any other band was just insane. I didn't understand that at all. It was a very strange thing, but if you look at the whole seventeen years of Phish, it was an exact angular rise. It was at the point where our manager used to be able to predict how many tickets we were going to sell in a given town based on how many times we had played there previously. Every time we played, it got a little bit bigger, and it kept getting a little bit bigger. I read a lot of articles saying that was happening, but I just didn't buy it. . . . I put Jerry Garcia right next to Jimi Hendrix. That's the level of importance I give him in my book of rock guitarists and American musicians. Jerry Garcia is an American musical icon. He's an enormously influential American artist. Part of the Dead's impact was they set up the touring-around-the-country thing. They invented a whole way of being a band, and obviously we learned a ton from them. . . . I know from being a Dead fan, if you were a Dead fan—a Deadhead—nothing's going to do it for you. If there's anybody that's going to discount Phish, it's people who are into the Dead. If you truly loved Jerry Garcia, there's going to be no replacement for him. Anybody who loves the Dead and comes out to see us is going to hate it. If you think you're going to get that fix, you sure as hell aren't going to get it.

Peter Shapiro: There was definitely a prebirth. I never went to Wetlands until '95–'96, so I wasn't even there. Ironically I will meet people who say, "I went to Wetlands in '90–'91 for Traveler and Spin Doctors!"—I wasn't even there! I was seventeen to eighteen years old then, living in uptown Manhattan, and never made it down. I went to Wetlands in late '95 and met Larry Bloch, who started Wetlands. I had been on tour with the Grateful Dead. When he decided to move to Vermont and live a different lifestyle and was looking for someone to continue Wetlands' mission, I raised my hand. I had been on tour with the Grateful Dead and I had been to Wetlands once, and I knew the importance Wetlands played in that scene. Then when Garcia died I spent a lot of time with the band. I knew there would be this yearning for people looking for music and the live experience, so I raised my hand to him and said I would love to help continue this, and I think there is more of a need now, with Garcia passing and the Dead probably ending, than ever before. I knew about the earlier-generation bands like Traveler and Spin Doctors, but I hadn't been a part of that. I was told I fit the bill well to take over Wetlands because I was naive and young and idealistic and still not jaded yet, and that is an important part of putting on shows—its stressful, it never stops, it has a lot of problems, things go wrong. So Larry Bloch, the owner of Wetlands, wanted to find someone that was still super-fresh. I was twenty-three years old, and he saw someone that was a clean slate when no one else saw that.

When Jerry Garcia passed away in August of '95, one thing it did was . . . with death comes rebirth, and I think for many years many people who were interested in improvisational music would just go on tour with the Grateful Dead. That is what everyone did in their early twenties and teens. When Garcia passed away it caused many people to explore new music and explore new bands to go see live. In '96–'97, that is when you really see the birth of the jam band scene. Wetlands, being this epicenter in New York City for that scene, saw an explosion of those bands. Seeing a lot of shows like moe., String Cheese, Gov't Mule, and the birth of the Disco Biscuits, I was fortunate to be at Wetlands and then take over in '96. So I found myself in the middle of it, and it really is a result of Garcia's passing and the Dead's pause, stop. But those people still wanted that outlet. They wanted to explore and enjoy live music. The Grateful Dead had a little bit of everything—they were the great American band. They had southern rock, jazz, blues, bluegrass, folk, so the scene has bands from each of those styles: String Cheese would be a little bit bluegrass, Gov't Mule would be a little southern rock, moe. would be Americana, Disco Biscuits would be a more electronica sound, and Phish, obviously, "the jam" in a classic sense. So in a way it all goes back to August '95—the moment something ended and something else began.

"Call Me Whatever
You Want—Just Call Me"

Perry Farrell [interview from *The Eagle*]: [The jam band] scene proves that the gathering force is the music, and it really lies outside commercial media and the mass media. This scene is grassroots . . . I feel it is a real part of the youth culture, and there is a real movement attached to it.

Reid Genaur: The music that forms me personally and musically is the grand- and forefathers of jam music: the Allman Brothers, Cream, Grateful Dead, Clapton—bands that jammed but mostly guitar-driven, seventies roots rock. The Grateful Dead were certainly the center of that, and they pulled that whole ethos through the seventies and eighties and into the nineties. Certainly there are many people that deserve credit, but for the sake of brevity, Phish picked up in the midnineties and continued that central jam band ethos culturally and musically. I dig it. That's where I got on the bus. I don't know where I fit into the spectrum, but at thirty-nine I want to hear mature playing. I wanna hear great musicianship and great songs. Phish has weird songs, frankly, but they're great because they are unique and original. You look up "jam band" on Wikipedia, and there is about 50 percent just filling the roll and the other 50 percent are really doing something that's cool, like Phish, or Les Claypool, or Keller Williams has his own thing. Those are just a few examples of people who take it and make it their own. Then there are people who do jam band stock 101.

Keller Williams: My take has always been: call me whatever you want—just call me. It's never something I labeled myself as. I think that's the beauty of the scene: you are what you are because the fans and people listening say you are. I would think the uneasiness of it is it's a pigeonhole people don't want to be put in, especially with mainstream media. It's like a bastard stepchild to the music scene. I think it's always been around, but the term "jam" really came the years after Jerry Garcia died. There was a longing, a void that needed to be filled, and these bands were branching out. I was definitely a part of that. I have never personally had a problem with it. You could call me alternative folk music. I don't worry about it, but I appreciate people coming to the shows.

Alan Evans: I got to the point where I accepted it, but I guess it's a very personal thing to everyone, and I feel like people are gonna categorize and call it what you want. But people are gonna come out to see it, so . . .

Eric Krasno: To be honest "jam band" means you defy category, because every single band I have heard with that label, they have so many different sounds that I guess it just means that you improvise. . . . So many bands are categorized that way, but they are such polar opposites.

Jim Loughlin: It means you won't hear this on the radio!

Vinnie Amico: I think it was a term they made up for bands they couldn't put in a genre. The name didn't exist until after the H.O.R.D.E. bands.

Rob Derhak: The jam band scene didn't happen in a town or a certain place. It was a national thing. It came about with a lot of the Internet, so bands were able to thrive in different parts of the country, but they had no scene name.

Chuck Garvey: It doesn't mean anything specific.

Rob Koritz: Yeah, living on the edge with improvisation for sure. Trying, striving to do something different without rehearsal. From a musician's standpoint that's incredibly risky—that is, to go on-stage to do something you may have never done before. It could work and be the greatest thing ever, or you could fall flat on your face. And it happens to jam bands all the time, if maybe just for a minute, but that is because they are going on that edge. To me that is what the whole jam band thing is about.

Steve Kimock: Personally my take on it was that the whole jam band thing showed up as kind of a slur on the live music scene by the big record companies who were having trouble getting people to show up for these boy-band concerts. Back in the eighties, when I first heard the jam band thing and it was like a derogatory term, I didn't agree with it because the band I was in then—and still—we improvise. But the way it was and is portrayed I think cheapens the whole thing. I think it's some marketing bullshit.

Jon Guttwillig [interview from *Heyreverb.com*]: We're an improv thing, and we're also the beginnings of a transfusion thing that we like to call super-jam bands. Normal jam bands—Grateful

Dead and Phish and Panic—are country jam bands. We're starting something called super-jam bands, where we're jam bands but
what we're doing is different. Yeah, and it's got a new edge to it. As
far as the new jam band that is playing super-modern music like
the Biscuits, who goes in there and who goes in the category of
jam bands? That's what we're striving to figure out.

David Graham: It's sort of a four-letter word, which is too bad. I
don't know why. Maybe it has the connotation of being soft, but I
think jamming is good. . . . When you say jam band all of a sudden
they relegate you to the Grateful Dead/Allman Brothers, and a
lot of people out there who just have a negative opinion of those
bands for whatever reason—whether it be politically, musically,
socially, or whatever it is—a lot of people have a negative response
to that. And I could understand that. I think it sort of means you're
not new. I think it has the connotation that "Oh, you're a jam
band. That means you play old shit, you're not progressive, you're
not modern, sort of lazy and old." That's part of it too. I have argu-
ments with younger people when they say, "Oh, I hate jam bands."
And I say, "Have you ever listened to them? You hate the name,
what it represents, but have you ever listened to any of those great
Traveler records or the live stuff?"

Joe Russo: I guess when I started playing more in the jazz genre . . .
I had moved to Colorado in '96 and met a bunch of guys that became this band, Fat Mama, that I played with back in those days.
At first that was like a party funk band, but then it started getting
into more of the experimental stuff like seventies Miles electric
band stuff and, in the eighties, the New York scene. At that time
we also started touring. I think our first tour was in '97, and I think
right around then was the first time I had heard the term "jam
band." Everybody knew about Phish and Blues Traveler and all the

H.O.R.D.E. bands, especially the East Coast stuff. So we are a touring band playing instrumental music, and we start hearing this term again and again. So we started to say, "Oh a jam band, like the Grateful Dead or the Allman Brothers or moe." It just started to encompass everything that was touring at that time. It felt like everybody that was improvising, whether it was based in country or pop or bluegrass or jazz, was now considered part of this jam band movement that was going on. Medeski, Martin and Wood was now termed a jam band. It was jarring at first for a lot of people that were coming from a different side 'cause, at least for me for a while, it was a dirty word—jam band. But more importantly the fans of jam band music, you start to realize they are into everything and they are so into it and they come to all the shows and they are really invested in what the band is putting out—and that was part of that movement that started to show me how deep it could go, and it wasn't just a term as much as an all-inclusive situation. I fought the good fight for a long time! Marco [Benevento] and I were doing the duo, and he didn't care, but I would always say, "We are not a jam band! We are instrumental postrock!" I've made my peace with it, and I'm happy to say I'm a jam bander. But that was the first crossover for me was the late nineties with Fat Mama and that term coming around. The first gig we did in New York was at the Knitting Factory, which was like our holy grail. Then we got a gig at Wetlands, and it was awesome. Then we kept going back, and we started going to the jam band festivals, like more of the hippie stuff, but again it was like this all-inclusive thing that was really cool. You could go see a hip-hop band or bluegrass or some jazz thing at the festival, and everybody was feelin' it.

Marco Benevento: Oh yeah, it's amazing—we had talks about this stuff while we were touring, and Joe [Russo] would say, "Since I was a kid I've always wanted to play Madison Square Garden."

And playing with Furthur he has fulfilled that vision completely. He is such an amazing person and a great musician. He has a really good ear, so he can really learn music intuitively quick. To see Phil [Lesh] and Joe hang out is cool; they have a good connection. Since then I have hung out with Phil at Phil's place, Terrapin Crossroads, sat in with them, then a week later played with my own band and Phil sat in with us. It's a great relationship!

Chuck Garvey [interview from *swaves.com*]: We definitely embrace it because we are a band that jams. We're an improvising rock band, or you can say we're a jam band and people get the picture. It also has negative connotations, maybe more so a few years ago, but at this point jam band has become such a wide variety of music under the umbrella of jam band, that it's not a very accurate way to describe things. You can say jam bands are part of the live music society, and maybe they improvise, but that's about it. It could be called bluegrass. Is Béla Fleck considered a jam band? The Disco Biscuits are a little more techno—are they a jam band? We're pretty much like a rock 'n' roll band that tries to write pop songs. There are a lot of variations on what a jam band is. So we embrace it because we are part of the live music culture, or the society that plays quite often in front of a live audience. It is what it is, and I think that's where music is at right now. And it's really just a tag for all these alternative bands that you won't normally find on the radio or MTV.

Béla Fleck: That's a tough one for me because a lot of people talk about properties of jam band music that I hear in so many other kinds of music. I'm like, well, jazz musicians jam, African musicians jam, bluegrass musicians jam. "Jam" just means improvising as far as I know. How many of these people are actually playing music unscripted with no structure? What is jamming? How much of it is playing in an existing structure that you have set up, and how much of it is actually playing completely free? Not too many people are brave enough to do that, including myself, because it's the riskiest thing you could do. Go out there with no framework whatsoever and dive off the deep end and hope something good will happen. If you have framework, like rhythm, then you have something you know will work. Improvisation is in so many different kinds of music, even classical music. They would improvise their own cadenzas. So if jamming is improvising, it's a problem. What's jam band music? I think jam band music has more to do with a connection to the Grateful Dead because it's a particular brand of improvising where the structure is based on structures that come from a certain time period. They are becoming modernized much as the way bluegrass has become modernized. Everybody takes the music they like and they build on it. So jam band music for me is a certain time period of people taking it to the next level.

John Medeski [interview from *Now Public*]: We have spent fifteen years trying to figure that out. We gave up. We call it MMW music. Our music is on the fringe of a lot of different things. We appeal to people looking for something different from the norm. We were called acid jazz, but that style solidified with a hip-hop base and we said, "We are not exactly that." Then the jam thing came, and we are not exactly that. We are not trying to play anything in particular; we are just trying to express and communicate—we don't think about it. We are dedicated musicians with discipline. The music we play doesn't sound like anything exactly. Maybe you can come up with a good name—there is a reward for that.

Tim Reynolds: Well nowadays it's expanded, in at least my mind. What the definition of it was, when it first came out, it was kind of the time I was getting into metal. I only knew of a few bands that were associated with that. Grateful Dead and other bands at the time, to me, were trying to sound like that, but over the years these festivals started incorporating bands of all kinds, and I got to know it's all about improvising with a lot of people. It's become a broader definition, like jazz. It expanded over the years. So many other things are too narrowly defined. It can be anything like Primus or Flaming Lips. I don't think of them as jam bands as far as the festivals that have been associated with that label as a word. When I was a kid in high school I didn't want to play songs—I wanted to jam. The sound of that back then was much different than that of what my first impression of jam band was, what it sounds like. I dig it now. It's so open.

Stephen Perkins: Well, Jane's Addiction started in '86, and then there was the alternative scene. Alternative to what, we're not sure; we were just into making hot sexual music, and all of a sudden it sounded different than what was happening. But to me alternative music was the Grateful Dead. Now when you think about jam bands, I guess you . . . it puts a strange . . . you don't want to categorize music at all, but at least you know if you're gonna see a jam band, you're gonna get some playing. You don't have to worry about a forty-five-minute set you saw last night. It's gonna be different every night. People are going to be coming and joining each other onstage, so at least it opens the door to say to the listener and the concert goers: "Be prepared for a musical experience. We are a community of musicians that like to play—take our songs further from when you heard them last or from the record." Like a great jazz musician, you have the top, you have a theme, and then you go. The word jazz came from jasmine, because the girls would put jasmine on in New Orleans and dance, and the whole scene smelled like jasmine—and that is where the word jazz came from. The word "jam," that's not a bad word 'cause when I was young I remember saying, "Let's go jam!" Not writing songs or learning someone else's song—let's just jam and find out what happens. Let's recognize that the category is full of players. To me Jane's Addiction was a psychedelic punk band. We love the energy and the danger and the honesty of punk, but we were also so into the psychedelic scene that we let that drip into our music. That's why we could do shows with Bill Graham. That's why we could be rubbing elbows with the Dead guys—because we had "Summertime Rolls" or "Classic Girl" or some other "take you on a journey" music. As a drummer sometimes I get stuck in rhythms, and if I get a fast rhythm and I'm eating dinner I will eat quickly, or while making love to my girl I'll be pumping quickly, so music really dictates what I do with my life. I've gotta be careful what I listen to. Punk rock would sometimes take me to a place I didn't want to go.

Mark Mercier: We built ourselves up as a "San Francisco sound"—whatever that is, I'm not sure. Scott [Murawski] was in the band before I was, and then he left, but I used to go see them, and I remember one night at the Rocking Horse in Hartford, and you [speaking to Scott] were doing "Sunshine Go Away Today," and in the middle you just started taking off on a D chord for about ten to fifteen minutes. That was the first time anything like that ever happened, and the crowd went crazy. Before when you did songs you might have a break or two, but to take off on something with no road map or without a progression to guide you was really something.

When we first started, because of the whole "hippie scene," there was an interactive scene, and there was a friend of ours that used to bring oranges to gigs and pass them out to everybody. People used to dance out the door and around the building. It was just a big convivial scene where it felt like part of the community, and then it went away. So we were playing, and people didn't appreciate what we did, at all, particularly in the Connecticut area. We almost got thrown off a stage at Central Connecticut University. They hated what we did. They wanted to hear KC and the Sunshine Band.

Mick Vaughn: I have run into so many musicians who don't like that label, and I guess my gut is, "Well, I don't really want to be called a jam band, but when you think about it, it's really kind of what we are." There are so many different kinds of influences coming into it. I wouldn't call us a jam band, but I wouldn't know what else to call us. It's a power trio. It's classic rock, is what it is. You could even call it jazz because when they are making jazz it's coming up with chord structures, mathematical equations, and then writing a head to it and then giving yourself an excuse to jam with your friends for ten minutes. The tune lasted for a minute and a half, and then for ten minutes you go wherever, and then the moment is gone. To me that is an ultimate jam band. Like to see Thelonious Monk play. He recorded the same song ten times, but totally different. He would omit things at the end of each song. To me that's jamming!

Michael Travis: I don't like that term, no, because I don't like the words together. It sounds like a pancake hitting a face or something. "Jam band"—it sounds so banal, and sonically it doesn't work for me. It flattens out a lot of what I think different bands are doing. It's stuck—I mean, you've gotta deal with it at this point. I think we step out of that class by doing such a smorgasbord of different styles that we try to honor thoroughly, like doing heavy-duty, actual salsa and then doing electronic music, and doing straight-up bluegrass, and straight-up calypso, and straight-up punk, that we're not like the Grateful Dead and Phish, although Phish was a great influence as far as pushing the boundaries and doing straight bluegrass songs, but they'd again soften them a little closer together. And we just have tried to really honor each style maybe a little more thoroughly than other bands in the genre. Maybe not. Maybe I'm just deluding myself, but . . . as opposed to the Dead, everything sounded like the Dead. He didn't pick up a different guitar; nobody was changing things to address styles . . . it was all just this kind of Americana-on-acid swirl-a-thon, same kinda vibe. They never pushed the envelope really. This is an incredible envelope, but they never punched all the way out to play a straight-up bluegrass song with an acoustic mandolin, acoustic guitar, twangy vocals, or a salsa song where the piano just keeps pushing, and now this whole electronic realm that we are entering into and just sort of organically developing. People hate us for it, but people hated us all the way since '95, when I added the drum kit and Kang added the electric mandolin. All of a sudden we were the worst band in the world for some people, and they quit seeing us and went away pouting, but we just have to. That is the most defining hallmark of String Cheese is that we'll always be a democracy and we'll always address whatever is feeling appropriate to make the six of us most satisfied musically.

Keith Mosley: I think I had more of an issue with it many years ago than I do now. It generally, to me, just . . . I don't even know what the "jam band" category means anymore, other than a band that doesn't play the same set list every night and is willing to do some improv on stage, take some chances, not come out with the polished show that you'll see every night of the tour.

Michael Kang: That whole thing . . . the reality of what that term means is different now because it's the tenth year of Bonnaroo right now. Bonnaroo back when . . . we played the first one and were involved in setting that whole thing up, and that was a real jam band festival that sold out before any advertising went out. And look at Bonnaroo now. The whole thing has really changed. The music industry, way back when, the jam band was almost like an alternative to the alternative. But it was noncommercial music in the sense that we didn't get any support on the radio or anything like that, except for Dave Matthews kind of blew that a little bit, because he is still considered a jam band even though he was not; he was completely mainstream. And I think for us at the time it meant we had our own publicity structure and how we put everything out, and it wasn't a commercially supported thing. Now there are so many different elements in how music gets put out to audiences. Arcade Fire's still arguably an indie band. They're not pushed as hard as some other bands and things like that. I think the music industry learns from bands like us how to succeed in making something that's going to last for a while. And yet there is still the commercial side to it. I don't really know what that term means anymore. It doesn't really seem to have anything to do with the music besides what people are . . . how they go about it . . . how they stay in touch with their own fan base and things like that. It's just, yeah, I don't really have a problem with it really, but I don't think it draws any boundaries for what the music actually is.

Tara Nevins: Give me a J! Give me an A! Give me a M-B-A-N-D!

Jake Huffman: I had never heard of a jam band until I was a freshman/sophomore in high school. I had listened to the Grateful Dead before, but I had never known. . . . It's like this secret society beneath the whole music scene that I had never heard about, and it's been in front of me this whole time.

Jason Ott: We don't go around saying, "We are the jam band, the McLovins." People just call us that. We are not going to agree or disagree. I don't like labels, but it is an easier way to understand. I think the label is more for the fans than the bands.

John Rider: I'm glad they came up with a term because we were trying to advertise way back when, and it was kind of hard to say what we do. We are sort of jazz and rock 'n' roll and sort of psychedelic and some country. When they finally came up with that term it was like, "Oh, okay, that's what we are."

Jeff Howard: I think what makes us a jam band is that rather than relying on the prewritten structure and song, we go off and don't know where the song is gonna go until we are playing it. We are spontaneous; we go in different directions all the time, and that is what the whole vibe of the jam community is all about— the song could be three minutes long or twenty minutes long, who knows?

Tim Carbone: Well, we were just talking about festivals, and if you go to a festival, you will see any number of genres that people are coming to see and enjoying and that they want. That is one of the things that attracts them to come to these festivals. So when you put a jam band tag on a band, like they'll call Railroad Earth a jam band and they'll call Umphrey's McGee a jam band and they'll call Great American Taxi a jam band. But the three of our bands couldn't be more different. A lot of the same people are enjoying all three of those bands. So it's got to be the fans; it's not the bands. It's people that like music that has room for exploration and good playing. I'm not saying we're the only band, but we're one of the bands, and there aren't a whole lot of bands that are more song oriented. We are a little more song oriented than your garden variety jam band.

Andrew Altman: When it comes to the term jam band, I like to count myself as one of the people who doesn't have my stomach turned when that term is used. There is a reason. It relates a lot to what Tim said. Musicians don't start out—or very few anyway—being called a jam band. None of them started out saying, "Let's start a jam band." Musicians in this world tend to be the type that are too confused to know what style they want to play, so they just get together with guys that they like to play with, and there is this sound that comes out. And that is one common thread that a lot of bands in our world share. It tends to run the gamut of feel and style, you know? It's a little funk, a little rock, it's a little bluegrass. It's just because we just can't decide, so we just do what we want. If people want to make it easy and describe it by calling it a jam band, that's cool. That's fine. It doesn't insult me because I just happen to be playing music that I like to play with people that are on the same page. Some people like to get offended by it. "We're not really a jam band, we're more of a . . . "

John Popper: It's been so advantageous and disadvantageous at the same time, so I can't complain. There are times I just don't feel like a jam band, and there are times that I absolutely do. I mean, it has to be called something. It's a flaw in Western thinking, in my mind, that you have to be able to compare a band to something to a . . . What does it sound like? It's like . . . or even if you're really excited it's almost like, "this meets that," like you have to make a Reese's peanut butter cup, you still need to define the chocolate and the peanut butter, there needs to be definition, and that's unfortunate. I think eventually something completely revolutionary . . . over time they start using the new thing as the thing to compare even newer things to. Someone will be the new Blues Traveler. You know, it will be that kind of deal, and then that person will be like, "I don't want to be the next Blues Traveler. I want to be the first . . . " Whatever they're called, over time someone will be the next. It's just that familiarity puts you at ease. That's really where it comes from. There is a psychological need to be near something familiar, and ultimately humans are familiar, so no idea is too different, too revolutionary. I mean, we're using musical instruments, for instance, you know? We still wear clothing, we sing words into a microphone; it's not like we come out and make noises like crickets and, you know, shit on the floor and develop hard exoskeletons and then dance around and make it rain and stuff. That'd be kinda cool, though, if we did.

Chris Barron: I love the whole jam band thing. I think it's great; I'm proud that we were there. I just don't want to take credit for something we didn't invent, and we didn't come up with the term jam band either. I don't think anybody from Spin Doctors, Blues Traveler, or Phish . . . I think somebody wrote an article on us in *Rolling Stone,* and I think it was like, the "hippie jam bands" or something like that, and that might have been the beginning of it. I don't even know if the term "jam bands" was even in that article. I think it came along a little bit later, but, yeah, we're a jam band. The thing is I'm not crazy about all the jam bands that are out there 'cause I feel like, for me, some of it's just not very song oriented. I like songs; I'm a song guy. We were always really interested in improvisational music—we had been to jazz school. Jazz is this improvisational music form based on this cannon of standard songs; there are great songs like "Stella by Starlight" and "Sunny Side of the Street" and these amazing songs. That's what makes jazz such a wonderful music form is that people would be like, "Hey, we're gonna play this tune," and play "Someday My Prince

Will Come"—Miles Davis—but we're gonna take it apart and put it back together musically. We were starting with a great melody, great chord progression, and a song that is saying something beautiful, so I think that's what we wanted very much to do, because I was interested in improvising, but I started out writing songs. We were all really interested in playing improvisational music, but we wanted to have great songs; we wanted to improvise the tunes that were great. I came into music, and my dream was, number one, to make a living at it and not necessarily be rich, but live comfortably, not to have to work for "the man," and, number two, I wanted to write people's favorite songs; that was always important to me. I don't have any problem with the term jam band being applied to Spin Doctors 'cause that's what we are, we totally are. And I don't mind when people say that we were influenced by Steve Miller and the Grateful Dead—you know, these are my heroes, I listened to those guys, I like those guys. I also listened to Thelonius Monk and other random stuff as well, but that stuff is maybe not—this motif—is not as evident in our music.

Warren Haynes [interview from *Concertlivewire.com*]: The same way that "Southern rock" is a limiting phrase . . . no one wants to be stereotyped or labeled. If someone looks at the phrase "jam band" as a genre of music that is full of open-minded musicians that play to an open-minded audience, then I'm all for it. But if you conjure up this musical image of endless noodling with very little direction and not too reliant on songwriting, then I don't think that applies to the Allman Brothers or Gov't Mule. In my opinion the whole jam band scene is an open-minded scene, and hopefully it continues to grow and become even more open minded. It should contain reggae music and jazz, bluegrass and rock 'n' roll and soul music and contain all genres of music as long as they have something in common with their works in progress and the people that are making the music are improvising and growing. You know, one of the big things in jam band world are bands playing a different set every night to keep their audience coming back, and I think that's a beautiful thing. I'm a big fan of songwriting, and regardless of a band's ability or desire to improvise really doesn't matter. There have to be songs that maintain your attention and prove some sort of timelessness.

Tim Bluhm: It's bizarre, we have been through different styles and eras. When we first started I think we were mostly psychedelic; it was completely unconscious. Most of what we do is unconscious. We are not trying to be anything, which I think makes it difficult. Our first record was very structurally psychedelic, not texturally so much, but the way the song worked and in the tempo changes, it was very unusual. It was the best we could do. Then we went into other periods where we were more pop with less soloing. Then we did a country rock thing, then we went to a Kinks kind of thing. I think most jam bands are pretty psychedelic, but that doesn't mean all psychedelic bands are jam bands. I think that's where people get confused. We are not a jam band—not that I care: it's fine if people call us that—but it's just been proven time and again that we just aren't. When we jam it's just different. I think we have a slightly darker thing, and it's not as danceable. I think for a long time being called a jam band was offensive to us, but it isn't anymore. We grew up. We figured there is no reason to be offended by it. It was our own insecurities. When you talk about the Grateful Dead, we got compared to them so often, but we were not familiar with the music. We got compared to them so often it became a source of tension. Then we did finally start listening to them and appreciating them and falling in love with that catalog of music. We had moments of "Oh, that's why they say we sound like them."

Larry Campbell: I don't know. I remember in the early seventies going to see the Dead and being completely swept up in what that was. It was a very unique mood of expression at the time, but I got to a point where, as a listener, it was too much. I wanna hear songs and a specific beginning, middle, and end expression. I was playing with Dylan for years, and we did a tour with Phil and Friends, and I sat by the side of the stage while they were playing. And that was the first time I'd been around that scene since going to see a Dead show in the seventies, and those guys were having so much fun, and I was starting to get what was going on, the communication that was going on. Then I had the opportunity to do some touring with Phil and get in there myself and realize that you've got a really forgiving and patient audience out there, and that's going to allow you to do and go wherever you want to go musically. I felt a sense of freedom that I never thought about before. Some of the people I got to play with while doing this, like John Scofield—who is one of the most generous musicians I've ever been around, but to be able to stand up there and play guitar with him and follow it wherever it was going to go and see what we could create just by talking to each other—it's a really cool thing. But there are moments of nonsense too—that's just part of it.

David Gans: I don't know. I think jam band is a moniker that was thought up by Dean Budnick in a moment when there was this kind of scene, centered I guess around the Wetlands, and there were a whole bunch of fresh new bands playing in that scene and appealing to that kind of Deadhead hippie fan thing. I've only met him once in my entire life, and I was in the first edition of the jam bands book, but that was all happening on the East Coast, and I was isolated in my own world out here with the Grateful Dead. I think it was a smart thing and he was trying to promote, I think, that scene. But look at the bands that were part of it:

Blues Traveler, Spin Doctors, a whole bunch of bands that have already disappeared. I guess Phish was all part of that and Dave Matthews Band, you know—those bands don't have a lot in common. What they had in common was the venues that they played and touring together and playing on certain festivals together. I guess the H.O.R.D.E. was kind of a jam band festival, which I never saw, was never part of. . . . So I think it was a convenient term to link together a bunch of musicians that were friendly and coexisting, but I don't think it is a descriptor for a style of music at all, because really most of the bands that fell under that label weren't really jamming. I mean, long funk grooves, extended solos—they're not jamming. That's not what the Grateful Dead were doing. When the Grateful Dead were doing it the Grateful Dead were truly creating something new every time they got onstage. The Grateful Dead fell out of doing that; certainly by the eighties I think the Grateful Dead had become a great sort of a stadium band, blues-based, but had roped off their improvisational passages into very small areas of their show. They were still keepin' it fresh, and they were playing their songs differently each time, but they became infinitely more consistent, infinitely more predictable, and infinitely less adventurous over time. Bands that were inspired by the Grateful Dead would take different pieces of what they liked about the Grateful Dead. Very few people could do it all because there was only one Jerry Garcia. You would take the long danceable groove thing and run with that, or you would take the great American song book aspect and run with that, or you would take the ragged but right vocals and run with that. There are a lot of aspects of Grateful Dead music; nobody had them all. I remember standing in front of Railroad Earth in Jamaica in, I guess it was 2005, and listening to John Skehan and Tim Carbone trading licks on "Seventh Story Mountain" and thinking that was as close to the Grateful Dead thing as I'd gotten since before there stopped being a Grateful Dead. 'cause there aren't that many musicians that are really listening to each other and creating spontaneous structures before your eyes and genuinely going out into uncharted realms. And I think a lot of the bands that fell under the jam band label were never that, were never ever gonna be that, and didn't even pretend to be that. I don't know what String Cheese called themselves in terms of their . . . no, Leftover Salmon was "poly-ethnic Cajun slam grass," which is a great name. But notice the word jam doesn't appear in that label.

Marco Benevento: There is a stigma with almost every style of music. There is some stuff in both jazz and jam that I don't like and don't want to listen to, but on the other hand there is stuff in those categories that I love. Even with rock—some I like, some I don't. There are stigmas with all styles of music as a musician, as an artist, someone who is just writing music. Now in 2012 there are a thousand names for song styles compared to twenty years ago. In a way you just have to get over it and say, "sometimes my stuff is jammy and we play in a certain key and we go there for a long time." But at the same time John Coltrane and Elvin Jones and Jimmy Garrison were jamming in E minor for a long time in their songs too. Jazz style. When we go into the improvising world I feel like our music leans more towards the rock side of things rather than the noodle jammy kind of thing that you would hear about. I have basically learned to get over the fact that . . . I think it's unfortunate that the jam tag comes with an almost negative connotation because it's just a word. Jam bands have expanded their definition, their umbrella, just like jazz bands have.

Jay Blakesberg: As far as I can tell the term jamband came from Dean Budnick, the editor of *Relix* magazine. Dean is a filmmaker and also a great writer/editor. It's a weird word but very appropriate. I know a lot of musicians don't like to be called jambands. Phish doesn't like it, and they are the king of jambands. Personally I don't think it's a bad word. I think bands that play music that's different every night, the ones that are taking chances, are the ones that are jamming. That's when you have an opportunity as a musician—I'm not a musician—but to me as an artist, as a photographer, when you're taking chances you have the most opportunity to be creatively brilliant, and if you're not taking chances and playing the same way every night on a tour, your opportunities to create magic are few and far between. So bands like moe., who are epic, they take chances night after night and sometimes you don't pull it off, but you're more likely to. Jazz musicians jam; Miles Davis jammed. It's weird that people are afraid of that word—it's an interesting word and I understand why, because it becomes affiliated with a certain type of fan or festival—but I think it's a valid word. It fits well, and I think it works for bluegrass and it works for rock bands and jam bands and jazz artists in so many ways. I don't want to see the bands I like play the same thing the same way night after night; it's just not as interesting.

Tara Nevins: Jam band, the definition, if there even is a definition, has certainly loosened. Because I think when it first came out, it seems like it was two things. One, it looked and sounded like a lot of it was mainly like bands that played these extensive, extensive jams. It was more about the jam than the actual body of the song, like verse, chorus, or lyrics. It was more about the jam. The little bit of lyrics were just a jumping-off point for the rest of it, which was really like jam for a really, really long, long, long, long time, and maybe come back at the end. And that was to greater or lesser degrees. And that was one thing. But the other thing was that it almost seemed like bands that you didn't know how to categorize were thrown into that. I know we were. I was down at Red

Light Management down in Charlottesville with the Dave Matthews crew and that whole team down there. I remember talking
to them with one of the guys in the office there about the whole
jam band thing, and it was kind of more like he couldn't categorize us. We are hard to categorize. What are we? You can't just say
rock. You can't just say folk. Oh and he also said, not just bands
that are hard to categorize but also bands that tour constantly. The
jam band definition seemed more narrow in the beginning, and
we would go to these jam band festivals and it seemed like, and
we could be wrong—this is not casting any kind of dispersions
or anything—but it sort of felt like the audience was really into
getting high and getting lost in these jams, which . . . that's cool,
that's totally cool. So I don't know if that is part of what the definition is about. Maybe it's about taking the journey of these jams
and getting high and kind of experiencing this thing, which is cool
because music is an art form. That's great. I think it's totally great.
That initially was more like that, but really over time it has way
broadened out. And it's like, we jam. We are of course very song
oriented, but we jam in many of our songs. Maybe not as long as
other bands. Maybe more tonically or less tonically or more dissonant or less dissonant than other bands might jam. But we jam.
We step away from the thing and the form. Some bands step away
from the form more than others, and it's all jamming. The Grateful
Dead—they were definitely a jam band. But they had great songs.
I think it's a very vague term. In a way at this point it's kind of
hard to define. It seemed clearer in the very beginning that it was
a certain movement towards this jamming sensation. And now it
seems to have stepped back a little from that and gone this way.
That's sort of how it appears to me. We've been on all these jam
tours. Del [McCoury] was on a jam tour. I mean, so what's that?

Mark Mercier: In a couple of ways the drugs people have taken have determined the direction music has taken, and the advent of ecstasy has developed a whole new set of hypnotic music that has to have a particular rhythm to it, the drum beat you hear all the time. It's hypnosis. Jam band music is a little more carefully constructed, and then you have the country element, which is just getting together to play. But Americana has come back. I think people are into the simplicity; they want a song they can hear and sing or hum in their car. It's more emotional than some of the electronica out there.

Jeff Lloyd: I was invited to do this press conference panel for Langerado 2007, and it was Modest Yahoo and Toots and Taj Mahal and David and Cesar from Los Lobos. Toots never showed, but I was kind of the guy that was lucky to be there. We were the local band that kind of snuck onto the bill, and that was why they had me there. And the question they asked Taj was about the whole festival scene—where he believed it had its roots and where it all came from. He had a really interesting answer. He was very clear and said it was all about the Grateful Dead. I was kind of surprised to hear that, but at the same time I believed him. That's what Taj said, so sure. I grew up listening to the Grateful Dead through friends. I'm from the northeast, and I grew up listening to Phish, and the Dead came later for me. It took me a few years to understand why everyone drew comparisons. I guess I understand it more now, but I'm not really sure. It's more about the whole festival thing and the whole audience—not so much the music. There is certainly the improvisation aspect of the music—certain things are the same—but just about everything else is completely different.

Taj Mahal: The Dead proved that a long time ago. Connect with your fans, and that's all you have to do. You don't have to play the corporate hit machine; you're a hit with your people, they will support it. Yeah, I would say that. They got out there and had national and international appeal and mystique. They had an incredible following.

Mickey Hart: We could only do it from time to time. It's not for everybody; it's really rare to fly without a net. We had an audience that allowed us that. It takes a long time to get into the trance, and when you learn the skill of playing in crowds, then you just think of how many complex systems have to come together as one to make transient music. It's almost impossible. Some people get hints of it and some people don't know what the real thing is, but when it hits you, you know you got it, and you want more and keep coming back for more. That is what keeps us coming back for more. And this is a big trance band [the Mickey Hart Band]. It loves the grooves, and it's fresh. It's like the Grateful Dead when we were young. You just learn how to jam. This band now is just being born, so it's fresh. It will get older and perhaps it won't have the spontaneity, but it's a matter of how long the audience can come with expectations.

Mark Mercier: Whether they appreciated us or not, most of them did come to see us at one point or another. I remember a quote by Guster, who is big now, and one guy would talk about how "Every Wednesday he would travel to Providence to hear Max Creek play." So we influenced them one way or another, even if it was what not to do. We always had a good number, a good enclave of appreciative people. And they would be from weird areas, like a couple girls from New Jersey who would bring hair dryers to Camp Creek, and then you would get hippies from Western Massachusetts. It wasn't necessarily a huge group, but they were always appreciative. They followed us around!

Tim Carbone: Well, the elephant in the room is that when you are branded a jam band, then when someone from the mainstream wants to talk about you, there is an element of looking down their nose. Musicians ultimately want to be as successful as possible. No one wants to be living in abject poverty for the rest of their life. A very large portion of being a musician involves living in abject poverty. They view the fact that you have to be accepted by the mainstream media in order to be successful. That may or may not be true. There is a part of me that kind of believes that, but then again I'm starting to let go of that whole thing. Let's let it ride and see what happens, you know? I think a *Rolling Stone* magazine or a *Mojo* magazine or any other one, if they look in any of your promotional material and they see that you are somewhere described as a jam band, then the door is probably going to be harder to open. It may not be completely closed, but that's just how it is. Let me put it to you this way: last night we played for 450 absolutely out-of-their-minds people who were over the moon about what we were doing. We were having a great time. Now at any given time, at any given club in Syracuse, where an alt band was playing and they were getting written about glowingly, by *Spin* magazine or whatever, and they were the next media darling or whatever, and I guarantee you go over there and there are 150 slackers staring at their shoes watching these guys. Not all the time. But what I'm saying is that if you are going to give me a choice, I will take 450 really enthusiastic people going nuts over what you're doing.

John Skehan: I think at the core of it, it's about the audience. It's the audience that has a really strong sense of participation in the music. I don't know if that is because of the improvisational nature of the music—they realize they are hearing something that they won't hear again the same way—or the fact that the repertoire is larger and more varied from show to show and night to night. But as you pointed out before with the explosion of festivals over the past ten years or so, you have large numbers of people out there that really shape their vacation time, their down time, around seeing live music, whether it is hopping on a tour for a week or going to a four-day-long festival, which, as you know, is quite an endurance mission. But they want to go to a place where they can intermingle with other people, see a wide variety of music, and come away with the sense that they have participated in something unique. They really do thrive off of that live experience as opposed to, let's say, the casual concert goer who is going to go to the stadium or the dome once a year to hear his favorite band come through and do their album tour and then go home. There are people who thrive on this, and they plan their whole summer around it. They really take part in it. The only other place I've seen this outside of this genre, although they are becoming quite intermingled, is in the bluegrass festival circuit, where everybody there is probably a picker or at least has a pretty strong historical knowledge of the music. When hearing all these different bands they have a frame of reference and background. They are very knowledgeable of the roots, of the origins of it, and who is on that scene now. It's the only other place I've had that strong participation vibe from the audience and the musicians.

Stephen Perkins: Open-minded concert goers, open-minded listeners of your music, and these people are willing and able to take it, and they want to hear you take them down deep and up high. They want tiny rhythm, like a cricket, and they want huge ones, like a boulder, and they are open for that. I think if a jam band goes jazzy, they are listening, and all of a sudden they get tribal, they're dancing, and then if the singer wants to tell you a story, they are gonna listen 'cause they know there is something to be said. I think that folk element is great when you have a story to tell. I think the audience has to be open to that. I'm at my best with Banyan, and we set up drums up front 'cause we don't have a singer, and I'm going off and I open my eyes and people are just into it, and I start playing better. Like when you see the Dead and they are getting louder and louder and it's getting more aggressive and they keep going, and the soundman is pushing it and everyone's pushing it, and I love that 'cause everyone is there for that reason. There are a few shows that I will leave my friends for and go to the pit. You just can't experience that in a seat, whether it's Pantera or something more jazzy. Just to experience that. I'm open to the ride, and so are the audience, the listeners, and if you give it to them, they are gonna want more.

Taj Mahal: The people—that's what it is! This is a crazy economy, and we've created our own space that even when things are bad, we have a place we can gather and have a good time.

Béla Fleck: I think that another element to the jam band scene—they're real people playing real music, not necessarily about a big show, lights, costume changes, or raw emotions . . . you know all the stuff that makes a good show. People were making a decision not to do that and do something more real, which was cool about the Dead, the grandfather of the jam bands. The Dead, to me, that is where so much of this stuff came from and the influences over so many bands over the years, not just themselves but what they did and the idea that you don't have to sell a lot of records to be a success. It can be about a groundswell, an audience that just . . . a place to go, a place to be, finding your people, that sort of thing. We have that kind of finding your people at bluegrass. There is a really strong scene right now; there are so many people playing bluegrass. I mean, they're having this renaissance right now. They are having the kind of time right now that some of the jam band guys were having in the early nineties. They're all finding kindred spirits and love a lot of the same music and are propelling each other and competing with each other to see where they can push the music and how to find their own personality in it. That's a beautiful thing when that happens, but I would say that's a syndrome, a really nice syndrome, which happens on occasion in the world throughout the centuries. I think the sixties was like that—everyone was spurring each other on to do better and inspire each other. Like, "Did you hear the new Zeppelin record or the new Yes record or Ravi Shankar or Hendrix, holy cow." That's a whole new world over and over again all in a short period of time. So I think all those people were coming up with a lot of the same influences and all having their minds blown at the same time by some of the same things, then growing up, doing their own music, and finding a way to be the next community to have an impact.

Ivan Neville: Absolutely, it goes back to the Neville Brothers playing with the Grateful Dead. There was always a connection. I look at San Francisco, and they kind of have a kinship to New Orleans, and New York as well. So there were some places that were ready and waiting, and we have evolved as a band. Our music has a lot of spontaneity involved. We do play songs that have structure, but we do a lot of vocals, whereas a lot of bands that would play our type of music would play mostly instrumental stuff. But we do vocals, so we do a lot of twists and turns. It's all about the energy, all about the crowd—that's what makes this music what it is. For us, depending on how people react to it, we play for the crowd's response.

Reid Genaur: This "catchall" covers a large spectrum from bluegrass to country to middle of the road—not middle of the road, but central—jam band to funk to electronica . . . it's a whole spectrum. I think that's something to be proud of, and it gives the scene a lot of elasticity and momentum 'cause there are so many bands that can play to that aesthetic or that community. I think the audience is more forgiving and more accepting and more open in those terms.

Steve Kimock: I think the thing is the community aspect of it. The whole idea of being live music and to participate in that is an important thing. I talked earlier about things as they are together and appreciating the history of the music. As you go back in time, things get specialized, and all the gathering stuff is just what people do anyway. Look at tonight: it's sort of a twenty-first-century version of the same old thing. You get the kids to bed and have a drink, a smoke, you dance around, and you sing. And in the morning you get the kids up and go to work and do it all again. At the end of the day, people getting together—that's what it is.

Dean Budnick: Although I am sometimes credited for coining the term "jam band" (for better or worse, often the latter, but it's all cyclical), I won't take credit. What I will say is that I certainly popularized it with a book and then a website of the same name.

On the other hand, I will indicate with full confidence that I was one who recast "jam band" as the one word "jamband." Now is that a distinction without a difference? Perhaps, although my intentions were sincere in both instances.

As I look back, it was initially an example of the tail wagging the dog. In 1997 I sold what would become my Jam Bands book to a publisher via a phone call after he contacted me to ask my advice about an altogether different matter. Then when I began working on the project my focus was the content, not the title. As I remember, I originally wanted to call it *H.O.R.D.E. to Handle,* centered on the bands that appeared on the various H.O.R.D.E.

tours. It then shifted to *Jamboree,* but my wife talked me out of that one, explaining that for her, the word evoked memories of Girl Scout gatherings. I briefly considered a title that employed such terms as Gobi, which the Ominous Seapods used for improvisational rock groups, or even Neo-Retro, which I always associated with Widespread Panic's Dave Schools and Blue Traveler's Chan Kinchla. But ultimately I landed on jam band, which many of us in the northeast had long invoked to describe such acts. Then the book was published, the website became popular, the groups it covered gained notoriety, and jam band stuck.

So while to some degree it all began as happenstance, in 2003 I had another bite at the apple. At that point I signed a deal for what was not quite a revised edition of that initial book but rather an altogether new take on the same general subject. This time I had the luxury of forethought. While I couldn't all out change the term itself because it had entered common parlance, I did think I could aim for a slightly more elegant take on it. I felt that jamband as one word was a bit more graceful, as opposed to proclaiming, "Hey look at these bands—they jam, they are jam bands." I also liked the fact that it was a neologism, characterizing what I felt was a new style of music.

So what does it all mean anyhow? Well, when I put together the program for the very first Jammy Awards in June 2000, I wrote, "Please cast aside any preconceptions that this phrase may evoke. The term, as it is commonly used today, references a rich palette of sounds and textures. These groups share a collective penchant for improvisation, a commitment to songcraft, and a propensity to cross genre boundaries, drawing from a range of traditions, including blues, bluegrass, funk, jazz, rock, psychedelia, and even techno. In addition, the jam bands of today are unified by the nimble ears of their receptive listeners."

I still feel that's true. While the term certainly references the dynamic, improvisatory nature of these bands' performances, there is a bit more to it. That other defining element is a penchant for blending established genres. For instance, Phish isn't a bluegrass band, a jazz band, a blues band, or a funk band or an electronic band, although at a various moments in their career and at a given moment in a particular show they might present music in any of those styles. Instead, they meld and intermingle those forms. They are a jamband.

I also understand that few musicians wish to see their art reduced to a one-word description, as this feels limiting. But sometimes shorthand is useful. While the term jamband may not be sexy or ironic, it does feel apt.

Plus, while we're on the subject of definitions, just what does jazz mean, anyhow? Alternative? Indie rock? At the end of the day it's all about the music anyhow.

Let your ears be your guides. Mileage may vary.

Travelers and Thieves

John Popper: As we toured nationally we ran into other bands that were doing the same thing. But the thing is, what I always said about the jam scene is that the bands aren't the same. I don't think we have anything in common. Like what Phish does is so different; I look at them as Classical geniuses. Trey is kind of like my Mozart—really my Bach . . . I think he would prefer that. What Widespread Panic has is cult-like! There is a connection between their audience and them that is . . . Phish has that too, but Widespread is unbelievable. Dave Matthews I think has done the most of any of us 'cause he has a little of that cult-like following, a little of the jam thing going, and a ton of pop success. He also has that Springsteen thing going. I mean, that guy can pretty much do whatever he wants. I say Dave Matthews was the smartest of all of us. Or the luckiest. You know, that's the thing—I don't really discern between smart and lucky, 'cause what's really the difference? Let's say you have a capable brain—that's lucky anyway!

Tim Reynolds: I don't know all the facts and all the details of all of it, but my general impression was when they [Dave Matthews Band] started and the band formed they had management already in place. A lot of bands starting out take a while to get management, and there is that whole arc of building on that basis, but they immediately had management . . . so it's kind of starting with complete smart planning. They immediately had a crowd and just built city by city and state by state. In a couple of years it went from nothing to everything in their arc. At one point they did a Grateful Dead tour, and they opened up for a lot of big bands, which pushed it more. It was really smart management in terms of merchandising and expanding fan base. I've always watched that from the side lines, and I was like, "Wow, that is pretty impressive!" It's the luck of the draw with the band and how people receive it in the larger public, but they obviously had all those elements going for them. They just kept moving forward.

Chris Barron: Along comes Nirvana, and I remember Nirvana was like a year or two before we started to tour. When we started to tour we would be going to these places and playing for, like, eleven people. Nirvana would have come through two nights earlier and packed the place. We're seeing that poster of the baby with the dollar on the hook. I was over at somebody's house, and somebody was playing some music and I was like, "What is this?" and they are like, "It's Nirvana," and I was like, "Oh, this is Nirvana? Wow!" I never owned a Nirvana record, but I always liked them, admired them and Pearl Jam . . . but that's a whole other story. But that cracked radio wide open and the business wide open, you know what I mean, 'cause nobody would have given Nirvana a chance two years before. But suddenly they come out with all this crazy, wild, angry shit that just exploded and blew the door wide open—and the jam band scene kinda snuck in after. But the cool thing about Blues Traveler and us and Phish was we were happy, positive, and funny, and my criticism, my friendly criticism of grunge is that it doesn't take a genius to point out that the world is screwed up and an unfair place. It's not a philosophical leap to be like, "Yeah, the world sucks!" People get treated badly everywhere you look; it's a dark, dark place, this world we live in. But it's another thing to try and take it on and bring a little happiness into the world.

Jim Loughlin: The Buffalo music scene was really awesome at the time. You could go out every night of the week and see every kind of music. Aside from the bands we knew, there were the Tails (more of a pop band), there were metal bands, hip-hop bands.

Al Schnier: There is a thriving jazz scene in Buffalo, great acoustic music, so much great stuff, like all the Dead bands that played in Buffalo. And because it's the second-largest city in the state and all of the college students there, it was on the circuit for all the national touring bands that would come through. And last call is 4 a.m., so there was live music all the time. It was a great place to grow a band.

Vinnie Amico: So many bands would play together because no one had enough music to play until 4 a.m.

Chuck Garvey: We played with a bunch of different weird bands. We played with our friends who were in Monkey Wrench, a kind of punk band, and one of our first shows in a bar was with them. We opened for the Mighty Mighty Bosstones once. We had a bunch of different styles of music that we were covering, so maybe that was one of the reasons we could do that.

Al Schnier: Some other bands we would play with are Scary Chicken, who was more of a college rock or an indie rock band at the time. It was a wide variety of stuff, and it was all with guys we were friends with. If we didn't have a gig, we were at each other's house drinking a beer or we were all at each other's shows and sharing gigs.

Rob Derhak: Some of the bands we've mentioned, like Monkey Wrench and Scary Chicken, had this great shameless self-promotion to everything they did; that's how we learned we needed to flyer and do all these . . . I don't remember if they started a mailing list or we did, but that was the thing that caught on. They used to give out tapes of their show, so we started doing that. We copied a lot of stuff that seemed successful for them 'cause we were just trying to learn what to do—things like having a connection with your audience, not just getting up there. There was a "just 'cause you're on stage does not mean you are any better than anyone else here" kind of attitude in Buffalo because it's such a blue-collar kind of town.

Al Schnier: It became a combination of out-drinking your fans and being able to be the last man standing in the bar as the lights went on. So much great music that came through, whether it was ska bands or whatever . . . we even got a lot of people from Canada, with it being so close. So we would see bands like Crash Test Dummies and Barenaked Ladies—all these bands that came across the border and were just playing in clubs at that point. It was great to be a part of that scene, and seeing those bands when they were at that level had a big influence on the music scene in Buffalo.

Keller Williams: The String Cheese story is: I saw them at Telluride first in 1995 as a postshow in a tiny little bar. I think they were a four piece at the time. I was blown away and went to see them in several other towns. After seeing them five to six times I gave them my CD and told them I'd be happy to open for them for free. I became friends with Keith. In the winter of '96 I got to do my first show opening for them, and in the spring of '97 I got to go on tour with them. We started at the West Coast, went up and across, and by the end of '99 I'd done probably one hundred shows with them. We put out a record called *Breathe* around that time. The whole ski pass thing came from moving to Steamboat Springs in '95, which was around the first time I saw them. I said I would play for $50 and dinner every Thursday—and a ski pass would be great—and I pulled that off for two seasons. Those two years I was in Colorado I was probably playing six nights a week at little restaurants, bars, and coffee shops, making just barely enough for rent, and by the time String Cheese allowed me to open for them I hadn't played a lot of places with a stage. They did amazing things for me. They got me the national exposure I hadn't had at that point yet. I owe everything to that band!

Michael Travis: As far as kindred, "ringing our bell," the two biggest influences early on are Leftover Salmon, and Phish, absolutely, was a monstrous influence, at least on some of us. Some of us didn't care, but me and Mike Kang were straight-up obsessed with Phish and have no problem saying that. I think they are one of the seminal rock 'n' roll acts of all time. Their jam style I didn't feel like we were as influenced by, but their songwriting and their presence and what they did. How they brought the community together . . . like having a chess game that was continuously going through the whole tour and the bouncing ball game, where each band member had a ball and every time it hit the audience they would play a note, and all these incredibly clever things. We were always feeling like we were playing catch-up to Phish in that way, not that we ever tried much harder to do it, but just constantly mesmerized by who they were and Trey's immense spirit. You know, Phish is the only band that has ever made my musical life do an exact right-angle corner. Like I was just cruising along and I saw them in front of two hundred people in '89, and I immediately bought the *Junta* cassette and played it until all the words were worn off of it and it was barely recognizable. I'd play it for anybody. I played it myself one hundred thousand times. I'd just be wandering around the country, visiting friends, and I'd be like, "Okay, you have to hear this band, man," first thing. They were huge with Kang too—mostly us two. Grateful Dead was just a constant stream of influence running through us—more, again, me and Kang.

Jon Gutwillig [interview from *The Dartmouth Independent*]: A lot of kids who see the Biscuits, who see the trance fusion groups, they never heard Phish. When Phish came back I would be talking to some of the people at our shows, and they would be like, "I'm excited to see my first Phish show." I heard that multiple times. And every time I heard it I was extremely shocked. Because I've seen a lot of Phish shows, and I figured everybody's seen a lot of Phish shows. But not the kids! These kids, when Phish quit they were twelve! They were listening to G-rated Christina Aguilera!

A lot of kids were in a pop phase and just never got into a jam band phase. A lot of kids get into their jam band phase in college, and there was a whole generation of college students without Phish during that period. For us it's interesting that there are people who haven't seen Phish shows and have seen thirty-five Disco Biscuits shows. Never seen a Phish show. That to me is amazing.

Phish being part of the scene is interesting, because it takes away from our draw, to some degree, and on very important nights, like Halloween and New Year's Eve, they draw from our draw. But we keep getting bigger, which leads me to believe that there are just more people who want to be part of the trance fusion scene.

And I like to separate the trance fusion scene from the Phish jam band scene. Because the Phish jam band scene is a real rock-and-roll, country-based thing. It's less based around dance music, and it's a little more mental. Which is cool—it's just different. So I consider that to be "jam band." Then there's the trance fusion scene—STS9, Biscuits—dance-y shit. In my mind it's different fans. In my mind it's a different style of music. But with the improv and with the fact that all of us influence each other . . .

Obviously, Phish is a big influence on the Biscuits. I've heard people say that Biscuits are a big influence on Phish! Obviously, when they go into like a techno jam, and they do a Biscuit-y thing, it's influenced by the Biscuits. So we're all influencing each other, and the common thread is improv.

Alan Evans: The funny thing is I have never heard a Grateful Dead album or Phish album 'cause I didn't grow up knowing about them, but our manager with Moon Boot Lover was a Deadhead. I think starting in Moon Boot Lover we were surrounded with people of the Grateful Dead era. I don't really know their music, but this great love of music that surrounds this whole scene, all these people are descendants of the Grateful Dead and Phish.

Dave Schools: The first time I heard the Grateful Dead it was the early seventies. I heard songs like "Uncle John's Band" and "Sugar Magnolia" on Richmond, Virginia's local radio station, and I thought they were this kind of country band—good, catchy songs. Then I went to this white elephant sale that my school was having to raise money, and they had a bunch of eight-track tapes, and there was a copy of the *Skull and Roses* record. I was intrigued by the artwork; it was the most iconic artwork I had ever seen. So I popped it into my eight-track tape player and the song "The Other One" intrigued me 'cause it was like twenty minutes long and I thought, "This doesn't sound like any kind of country music I have ever heard before. I don't think I would ever hear this on the radio." It was a trip. I was in third or fourth grade, and it took me on a journey and I became fascinated. So over time I was able to get a paper route, save some money, and get some records. I got *Live Dead* 'cause it had lots of long songs. I figured, "Wow, maybe some of these side-long songs will go to different spaces." Sure enough, it turned me around, and it all led up to me seeing the Grateful Dead at the Hampton Coliseum in 1979 for the first time. I didn't really get it until it was 1981 and they were performing "The Other One." I was really into the Who and a lot of bombastic Sly and the Family Stone—I loved classic rock, and it was also pyrotechnic and costumes and light and glamour. Here are these guys that look like they are coming off the street creating this effect that was so palpable, simply through their music, standing there looking at each other listening and playing, and when it goes to another level, that is something you can't help but be affected strongly by. And there was Jerry peering at the rest over his eyeglasses and just weaving this spell. It was beautiful and that was it. I got it then. So I saw as many of those concerts as possible, mainly during my college days in the early eighties, and then I started a band and wanted to bring about the same spirit!

Stephen Perkins: When the Dead broke up and Jerry disappeared, things changed, and of course, Phish really pulled it out 'cause they are such great players. I think that's what happened. Their songs, their sense of humor, their scene—it's one thing. But their playing is what turned people on, and there was this youth that was a little bit dangerous. They're pulling weird stuff out of their hat, and it pleases people 'cause they want to hear it and they put their take on it.

Tom Constanten: I went to UC Berkeley as an Astronomy major in 1961, and I fell in the crowd of Phil Lesh and Jerry Garcia before they even formed a band, before they got around to doing that. It was natural that they would give me a call because we had this mutual music-admiration society going. I was sharing an apartment in Berkeley with Phil, and we drove to the peninsula and he introduced me to his friend Jerry Garcia. Phil was the big brother: he was twenty-one, and Jerry was nineteen, and I was seventeen. One thing led to another thing we couldn't predict, but we enjoyed the ride. Strangely enough you might think it's counterintuitive, but the thing is, from among my dearest, best friends at the time, Pigpen was the best man at my first wedding. We always got along famously even though our musical backgrounds were wildly different. He came from a Blues background. His father was a blues DJ on the radio called "Cool Breeze." He was surrounded by that at a young age. He obviously absorbed it in terms of his keyboard playing and his vocal presentation. There was nobody like him.

Marco Benevento: As a musician and someone who is learning music, you go through those phases where you need to find "bridge" music to get you to another level. Learning to play piano as a kid, taking lessons, then getting into rock and learning songs as a kid, and then you hear jazz and you learn about improvisation, playing over a C blues, you have to have an artist that bridges you over to that world. For me Oscar Peterson or Bill Evans, they brought me over to the jazz world from rock, and also a lot of the organ players brought me into that world, like Jimmy Smith and Larry Young. Then I saw this rock-jazz thing, this heavy jazz kind of thing, and that's when I was like, "Oh, that's how that can work!" I feel the jam world as a musician; if you're doing a lot of improvising and exploring in the night, you're gonna get into those worlds, those notes of jazz, just because you are learning that stuff as a musician. It's all about being a musician and expanding. It took me a while to actually like jazz, especially the saxophone. I feel like the jammers are the musicians who are searching always. They are gonna learn about jazz and Latin music and all sorts because it's all just music, twelve notes making songs! I think everything benefits from each other, but I do see the connection between jam and jazz for sure.

Larry Campbell: Phil [Lesh] has told me that Big Pink was a huge influence, especially on Jerry at the time, and that Workingman's Dead and American Beauty were very much influenced by what the Band was doing at the time. Which is why when we were doing Levon's [Helms] last record, I had just come off a tour with Phil and was trying to think if there were some songs that would suit Levon that came out of the Grateful Dead being inspired by the Band. And I thought about "Tennessee Jed." It's from that era and they never recorded a studio version of it, and I thought it would be interesting to see what Levon could do with a tune like this in a way that is sort of full circle. Here's the Band influencing the Dead, Jerry writes the tune, the tune is good, it sounds like something the Band could do. Rearrange it a little, make it to what would sound like a Band song, then Levon records it. I thought that was pretty cool.

David Gans: The Grateful Dead became the most compelling music that I knew. There are a lot of reasons for that. One, the music itself was pretty goddamn interesting at that time, and also the culture around it was very intriguing and attractive in a funny kind of way. It was like belonging to a secret society; the people that were into it were way into it and there was a lot of arcane stuff to learn and language. It was very compelling, and it was weirdly hierarchical and sort of addictive in a way to try to make your way into that scene, like any kind of secret society. You knew something that other people didn't know, and there was this tension between proselytizing it and keeping it for ourselves kind of thing, you know.

Rob Koritz: Because Grateful Dead music encompasses everything, that's one of the beauties of it. You are basically playing every style in the world in the Grateful Dead's repertoire. To me they are true American music. They've taken all these music forms, which are by and large true American forms, and play them together.

Dino English: I discovered the Grateful Dead late, but when I was educating myself as a drummer I wanted to be able to play all different styles so that I could hang if I got called for a certain genre of music—and I really enjoy all kinds and styles of music. So when all of a sudden I was exposed to the Grateful Dead in a big way it was, "That's it. All in one big package."

Jackie Greene [interview from *Glide* magazine]: The biggest thing for me is in the songs I've been writing lately; I've been taking a lot of influence from these Grateful Dead songs. In order to perform them a lot I've been studying them and realized how great they are. And so I've been influenced a lot by them, not a lot of the songs on this new record [*Giving Up the Ghost*] so much, but more of the songs you'll hear on the next record. And playing live with my band, we've started to stretch out more. The songs get a little loongerr. . . . We jam a little more . . . we're taking a few more chances. Phil has made me more comfortable with that; I was not comfortable with it at first: "Uh oh, that's scary . . ."

Chuck Garvey [interview from *Swaves.com*]: At the time we started doing it [moe.] the songs were bizarre and fast and not really extended. But in Buffalo the bars stayed open until four or later, so that had a little bit to do with it. But another aspect was we started traveling around New York State. Our first travel gigs were like Poniana, where Al went to school, and all of the small college towns in Upstate New York and Erie, Pennsylvania and Toronto. And basically, just to keep things interesting for us on a daily basis, we started extending the songs. Al was a really big Deadhead, and he said, "Why can't we start stretching things out?" It was really like if you have to play for three or four hours a night and you don't have a ton of material, you have to stretch everything.

Jeb Puryear: We're kind of from left field for some reason because a lot of people hear our stuff and they think we're, like, a Grateful Dead cover band that writes our own stuff. There are a ton of bands like that. But we never really listened to the Grateful Dead. And then there are a lot of bands that are just straight bluegrass bands and then they started adding electric instruments. But they play basically a bluegrass derivative. But we're not really like that. So as far as our lineage . . . our lineage is very strange. Basically we were playing old-time music and then started a rock band. Then we started writing songs. So in a way what we sound like is this natural mix of everything we listened to ever and liked and it just found its way in there.

Tara Nevins: Playing fiddle music, playing old-time traditional music. I was in a band, St. Regis River Valley String Band, and we came to Ithaca, New York, to play a gig, and Jeb and his brothers came to the gig. They were bored, had nothing to do, came to the gig, and they played the same kind of music. And you know when you play the same kind of music the old-time community is, that if you go to a gig and there are old-time musicians on the stage and you play too, you end up meeting up after the show and probably jamming and, you know, that kind of thing. And that's what happened. And we just all hit it off.

Trey Anastasio [interview from *NPR's Weekend Edition Sunday*]: I met him [Ernie Stires] eight or ten years ago. I was looking around Vermont for a working composer, and his name was mentioned by some friends. And I visited him at his home in Cornwall. He's a real character. He's just a guy that spends his days sitting at the piano writing music. And the first day that I met him he played. I heard some of his music and it was unlike anything I'd ever heard before. And it changed my life, I'd say, from that point on.

In twentieth-century classical music and in jazz one of the things that was happening was people were pushing the definition of consonant and dissonant. Whereas some of the things that sound dissonant at one stage of history begin to sound consonant as time goes by. So the vocabulary is being pushed. And he always works at the edge. And I think that's why it might sound sinister in a certain way.

But to me it's beautiful. And I think that's one of the things that's so amazing to me about him. It's as if he's truly writing for himself. He's truly writing music that he wants to hear, that he wants to exist in the world. And he doesn't really listen to critical voices. That's what makes him important as an artist.

Trey Anastasio [interview from *Charlie Rose Show*]: I think what made Phish unique—this is my theory and I think the other guys might chime in together on this one—there was so much composed music at the beginning, and that's why I say if you go back to the first album, listen to it, it's "Foam," "Divided Sky,"

"You Enjoy Myself," "Fluffhead," "David Bowie." Everything I just
listed are, you know, eight-minute-long, heavily composed tunes.

So what would happen is we would play these very complicat-
ed pieces, and then improvise. And what I found was that the improvisation was bent because of the fact that we had just coexisted
within music that was very tightly composed. So we were used to
being—if you played a four-part fugue, which we did a number
of them, with two halves of the piano playing the interlines, me
playing the melody and Mike playing the bass line, where everything was interwoven. When we improvised, our improvisation
was changing keys and going together like a snake, and I think it
made it a little bit unique to my ear, from other bands I had sort of
jammed with. Usually you have a band kind of strumming along
and one guy playing a solo.

Jeff Lloyd: My mother is a music teacher—that's where my roots
are. I grew up reading and playing music. Phish was a big one
for me. I went to my first show in 1995. About a year before that
I found music and immediately latched onto it as a whole new
world of guitar playing. What Phish did for me is they made me
believe—no, they taught me that a rock band can do anything
they want to do. Once they cracked open my head and put that
in there it's been nonstop . . . I'd never seen anybody write music
for a band like that before. So that just opened up this whole new
world of possibilities for me as a guitar player and as an adolescent
musician, it was just a huge inspiration, ya know, just limitless.

Reid Genaur: I think the tadpole of Strangefolk started in 1991,
and then the band was probably more like '93, and then we started
playing with real regularity in '94–'95. . . . Phish was on the rise—
that was inspirational musically, certainly, but also just in terms of
organizationally and emotionally. You are seeing someone succeed

by their own rules. It gave a lot of bands courage to go out there and do it because it felt viable. I know that's what the Grateful Dead did for years and there are a lot of other examples, but by the time I was a teenager the Grateful Dead were in their fifties, so it wasn't relevant. Their success did not give me inspiration musically. But seeing guys close to you in age and seeing it unfold literally in front of you was like, "Whoa, this is possible!"

Joe Russo: In the Fat Mama days we crossed paths with Soulive, Moon Boot Lover, Ulu, which is a New York band we played with quite a bit. Marco and I would also do a lot of work with the Slip, another band who at first was not aware they would end up a jam band. As Marco and I went on we kind of made a conscious effort to book stuff that normally wouldn't be considered as part of that scene, like pop bands or DJs trying to push it a little more. We brought out this band Something for Rockets from L.A., a total jam pop band. It was awesome! Working within the jam band idea, while still pushing it a little. I guess the duo years were my harshest years, but that is just being younger and dumb and cocky . . .

I owe a lot to Mike Gordon. Marco and I became friends with Mike in '04, and he would come play with the duo. Then Trey got wind of what we were doing with Mike and we went in and did a recording session for one of Trey's solo records, and that turned into, "Oh, we should do a gig." Then the gig at Mercury Lounge turned into a tour with Phil Lesh and Friends. We did that in 2006. It was Mike, Trey, Marco, and me; it was called GRAB. That is when I first met Phil, but it was very brief, but then we played together at Bonnaroo when the GRAB thing was announced. So years later I get this random call from Bob's manager, Matt Busch, leaving me a message, asking if I would have any interest in playing with Bob Weir and Phil Lesh. So I called him back and got sent five tunes about a month before this sort of audition, which I didn't know or think of it as that at the time. The tunes just kept rolling in, and soon it was up to sixty tunes. This started to really open me up to all this stuff the Dead did that I had no idea about. So I would learn these tunes and we would play at Bob's old studio, and we started a little band and started doing a couple shows at the Fox Theater in Oakland to see how it went. That was three years ago, and it's been pretty incredible. I am so very thankful to be doing this. I never would have thought I would be here, and it is a very humbling, exciting experience.

Joel Cummins: I've just been reading Keith Richards's book *Life,* and he talks about how in the early days of the band they were trying to emulate the Chicago blues. It's so interesting to see how it made it all the way over to England, and now they're selling it back to us. Chicago is so rich and so deep with that tradition, and to me, what it really taught me was that all of these cultures, be they jazz or . . . I went to see Kurt Elling and Ramsey Lewis over the years in Chicago. I grew up going to see Buddy Guy and playing in his club, and I got to play with Otis Taylor, who is a great trance-blues musician. At the same time you have Wilco and the Smashing Pumpkins, who are really Chicago bands, and you have groups like Tortoise, who were a big influence for us and that whole Thrill Jockey scene. You have a lot of different styles of music happening in Chicago, and I think that's another thing that really speaks to what Umphrey's McGee is about as we explore all these different hybrids of sounds. Of course Chicago House is another one where the style of club and dance music originated as well. It's exciting to see all this happening. To me, I think, it brings a greater appreciation for all this different kind of music, where you don't really have to put the blinders on and say, "No, I'm only this thing." It's cool to live in a place where this is all going down.

It's a great town. We wouldn't be the same band if we weren't a Chicago band.

Steve Kimock: Yeah, I really cut my teeth playing with the cats in the Bay Area. That is really where I learned. The trial-and-error band stuff is how I learned. Like Bobby Vega would say, if you're around people with colds, you're gonna catch a cold, or if you go into a room with people playing East Bay funk, you're gonna catch that. So if you're with people playing psychedelic R&B tunes like the Garcia band, you'd catch that. And I did. Which is a different musical thing to catch than the New York scene, which tends to be a lot pushier. There are obviously regional styles. There are obviously cats that are Tulsa and guys that are New Orleans and guys that must have something to do with Austin or North Miami, Seattle, Chicago—it's their scene, nothing wrong with that. I think that's great.

Taj Mahal: When I was going to UMass I had an R&B band, and we used to play all the Ivy League colleges, so I was building something up here. Then I got into this solo dual folk-blues thing, then went out to California, hooked up with Ry Cooder and Jesse Lee Kincaid and Gary Marker and Ed Cassidy and created the Rising Sons and eventually went on and did my own thing. The San Francisco people are the ones that really endorsed it. I'm glad I had an opportunity to work my way through it.

Ivan Neville: I look to, like, Sly and the Family Stone. Sly talked a lot about having a good time. But he did sneak stuff in there in subtle ways. The members of his band made a statement as well. He had a multiracial band in a time when you didn't see that a lot. He had a white guy on drums—that really hit me—and they had two girls in the band. They had a chick playing trumpet and a chick playing keyboard and another white guy on sax. They made a statement right there, plus they mixed rock 'n' roll and funk and blues and soul and gospel like nothing I've ever heard. That heavily influences me along with being from New Orleans and my uncle [Art Neville], who formed the Meters.

JoJo Herman: [interview from *Gonola.com*]: I think the first one [Professor Longhair album] I heard was *Crawfish Fiesta*. I was actually playing in a band—this was a long time ago, in the eighties. We were into ska music and bluebeat music. We had a lot of songs like that, like the Paragons and Toots and the Maytals. The bass player, Gary, he said to me, "You should check out this piano player Professor Longhair," because that's where all this music comes from. He gave me *Crawfish Fiesta*, and I listened to it. I'd never heard anything like it. I just became infatuated with it. On the instinctive level, just the way it hit me. As a piano player, it's like, "Wow, this is piano rock 'n' roll music." It's not where the piano is part of a guitar band, which is almost everything I'd listened to. This was just a whole other thing. The intricacy of the rhythms, rhythms I'd never heard. It was just so funky. I was just kind of drawn to it for all those reasons. 'Fess's songwriting too. The first 'Fess song I learned how to play, it was "Tipitina." Then I learned "Stagger Lee." Then I got into more Mardi Gras, second-line rhythms like "Mardi Gras in New Orleans," "Hey Now Baby." Those songs have that kind of rumba bassline. I just learned how to play that rumba boogie thing that 'Fess mastered—and created really. Yeah, different approaches as far as the basslines and the left hand go. I carry all that just on the piano—an acoustic, upright piano. I play a lot of Longhair. I learned how to play off of Pete Johnson, who was a phenomenal piano player. He played behind Big Joe Turner. He just created all those boogie lines. Just that piano boogie woogie he was so great at. I learned a lot of that. I'm really into Lead Lux Louis these days, and, of course, Dr. John, Mac Rebeanack. He blended and infused everything together, created the whole New Orleans thing.

Warren Haynes [interview from *Murf's Southern Steel*]: We formed, the original idea came back in '94, [Allen] Woody and I were in the Allman Brothers from '89 til April of '97, and in '94, while we were doing an Allman Brothers tour, we were talking about how nobody does the improvisational trio anymore, what a hard format it is to find the right chemistry for, and Woody said, "You know, me and you and the right drummer could do that," and I thought "Me and you and Matt Abbes could do that." Woody had never played with Matt. I had played with Matt, and having played with him and Woody both, I had an idea that they would be a really good rhythm section. So we started making plans to get together the first convenient day, do some jamming, and we did. The first time we played together was beyond even our own expectations; the chemistry just was really good. But then, as with any other band situation, you know the initial chemistry is a really important thing, but what can you do with that is probably the most important thing. The longer you can keep it together, the more you can build upon it.

Stephen Perkins: When I started drumming I was only eight, and my turn-on was jazz drummers. They had a chance to say something in the music. If the horn player got to say something, the drummer got to say something. It was lyrical, dynamic, and they would actually have peaks and valleys in the drum part. When Motown came around, the drummer became more of a clock, and the song and the melody took over. But then Ringo and Mitch Mitchell and some of the great rock drummers in Motown in the early days started getting that jazz feel, where they would communicate with the instruments instead of being a clock. That is when I started to get turned on even more, and that's when you can improvise. There is a certain feeling when you set the frame of the song and then you can go from there. I always found that once the board was set, people would feel either the pulse or the tempo or maybe even the esoteric "milkiness" of the song, but once it's in their brain you can start improvising and communicating with the other instruments. I always thought as a drummer that a lot of people don't hear melody in a drum. But I tune the drums very melodic to try and have melodic drum fills, just as a bass player, guitar player, or a singer would do, and that's where improvising lets me do my thing and not just be the clock. I want to communicate onstage with the audience. To me improvising just keeps going; it's changing the world still. The first improvisers, years ago—that music is still out there. I think when you improvise you are letting your soul out there, and then your soul is out in the universe, so what you said and felt at that time continues on. I was very lucky to play with Bob Weir at Rob Wassermann's wedding. I did some drums, and Bobby came up and we did some Dead stuff, but I felt like I needed to be a clock 'cause I wanted Bobby to rely on what I was doing. But I thought, "He doesn't play with a clock. He plays with improvisers." I had a moment stuck between giving Bobby what I thought he wanted or what he needed. That was a great moment in my musical career. I was nervous. It opened my eyes to improvisation.

Mickey Hart: Mysterium Tremendum means a lot of things to a lot of people. The ahhh, the wonder, the illumination of meeting the sacred—something that is larger than yourself. Also things such as the mystery of the birth of the universe, the Big Bang. Mysterium Tremendum could be interpreted as what came before nothing—from nothingness to something, the universe was born 13.7 billion years ago. The Mysterium could be thought of as what happened before nothing. It's open ended, infinite, like the universe itself. For the work I am doing now Mysterium Tremendum was about changing the radiation that comes from different epic events that happen in the universe. Everything in the universe that moves sings its own tune. Mysterium Tremendum is having some kind of conversation within the universe. The moment of creation—once we were able to detect it I wanted to hear what it sounded like. George Smoot won the Nobel for finding the cosmic background radiation, the remains of the Big Bang, so that is what Mysterium Tremendum means to me.

I don't capture the sound; I'm capturing the radiation using radiation telescopes. Once I gather those light waves, then you take that, put it into an algorithm, change its form into something we can hear, and use that to compose with. And that is what we are working with now.

Joel Cummins: Just the other night we did a four-night run at the Brooklyn Bowl and had some special guests, including Biz Markie and also the Grateful Dead's Bob Weir. It's just one of these things where we became friends with Matt Busch, Bob's tour manager, first, and Bob was on Jam Cruise with us this past year. We were talking about doing something in his TRI Studios, and it just happened that Bob was in the region for a gig with Levon Helm and playing up at moe.down with the guys in moe. So he was in New York with nothing to do, and Matt reached out to us and said, "Hey, would you guys be interested in having Bob come out?" We said, "Of course!" So Bob was down with it, and he came out and we played the Buddy Holly tune "Not Fade Away" with him, which is one of his more noteworthy vocal tunes with the Dead. He also learned and performed our tune "Glory" with us. So it was really a neat thing to have him up there with us; we had that cross-generational thing happening. Phil Lesh came out a few years ago at the Great American Music Hall and sat in with us there. That was another fun one because it was much more on the spot. We found out that day he was coming and didn't have time to talk about it or plan it, so we pulled out our cover list and he literally looked through the entire list and was like, "I don't really know any of these." There was like 150 songs on it. For some reason along the way we had played "Help on the Way," "Slipknot," and "Franklin's Tower" like two to three times just 'cause we wanted to learn them and we thought they were cool Dead tunes that spoke to our more progressive side. So he saw "Franklin's Tower" in there and was like, "Oh, I know this one." He says to Brendon, "Who is going to sing it? You?" And he was like, "I think you might know it a little better than I do." And Phil's like, "Okay, I'll sing it!" So we have had the honor now of Phil Lesh sitting in with us, Bob Weir played with us, Bill Kreutzmann sat in with us two years ago at Los Tortugas Festival out in Yosemite. So we have had the honor of sharing the stage with many great artists. It's a bit surreal to have some of those artists. I was in a college cover band singing "Not Fade Away" and then to be singing harmony with Bob Weir while he is singing lead on it was a pretty cool thing!

Béla Fleck: I think you have to be careful not to assume doing a lot of genre crossing makes you better. I think all of this is about being an artist and choosing your venue. So somebody who decides they're gonna be a traditional bluegrass banjo player versus someone who decides to do all kinds of things—one is not better than the other. There's just a choice of where you want to put your marbles, 'cause you only have this many marbles. So for me, personally, I figured out that I had an affinity for playing different kinds of music and it was probably one of the better things I could do 'cause there were a lot of people who did bluegrass really well and I could soak up a lot from different kinds of music, and then the idea that all these different musical experiences would lead to me being a more diverse musician so that when I'm creating my own music, I'd have more to draw on. So, like, spending a year on classical music—which doesn't sound like much when you think of how much students in classical music spend—or spending time with a great musician like Zakir Hussain doing Indian classical music. You spend your whole life learning how to play it, and I spend a couple years playing with him or playing with African guys for a few years or trying to play jazz. I couldn't do any of them enough to be one of those musicians, but I can take all those influences to become the hybrid musician I'm trying to be. Since my music is outside of those boundaries, I get to keep putting in influences. It's like a stock pot of stuff I keep putting in and the soup keeps getting richer and richer—hopefully it will still taste good. That's the key. That's where the art comes in—trying to make all that palatable, 'cause it could be a big mess. I've always liked the idea of being outside a particular genre.

Tim Reynolds: I think we [TR3] have all been into a lot of different kinds of music. We played music for a living and did other things, and music is such a beautiful thing, there is no reason to limit yourself to one style. To me the umbrella of rock music above and beyond other styles is that it brings it all together. The trio format gives it a certain sonic signature: electric guitar, bass, and drums. For me, I've been through many phases of hardcore—like a jazz phase, an acoustic phase—and at this point in my life I'm trying to draw on all of that and keep learning more about everything. I think both listeners and musicians, a lot of people are open to different styles. When I wrote "Kabbalah" I was first getting into Middle Eastern music. I can't remember if I was on the violin or mandolin, but I was infatuated with how Middle Eastern music has this microtonal edge. It gives it the vocal quality, all the instruments, and singing—especially in India. But that's where the song comes from. We play it like a rock tune, but it's that kind of music.

Béla Fleck: I maintain the thought that great music is always happening on the edge of genres, not in the center—or most interesting music anyway. Pat Metheny, for instance—he has a lot of different influences. He's influenced by Brazilian music. He's very influenced by rock. There's even a new age quality to his music. He's very influenced by mainstream jazz. So his music reflects all of those things. I think he also likes "out" jazz—for instance, that Ornette Coleman record he did—and he makes great music out of it, and that's his own music. Umphrey's McGee, I think they are taking from wherever they like, whether it be a trance vibe, a country vibe, or a jammy thing. Whatever it is, they write their own music, and it's really good and it's hard to put your finger on it. Sometimes the word "jam band" could almost seem like a negative to some people. Are they a jam band? I don't know. They are just a good band with a lot of diverse influences. The negative side of the jam band idea is the noodling, like the idea of Jerry Garcia on a bad day, or like long pointless jamming. Just because someone is jamming doesn't mean it's good. It's gotta be good. So Jerry on a good day is like, "Wow, I really like this music!" But I remember talking to people [who are] saying, "Yeah man, I've been to the last twenty Dead shows and Jerry hasn't been on—it hasn't been happening!" I'm like, "How many Dead shows are you gonna go to before you hear one you like?" But it doesn't matter—that's their community. That music is the lifeblood for those people, and it doesn't matter if the guys are on or not. So I think that's an interesting piece of that whole scene. People fall in love with their music, the music of their time.

Justin Carrey: I would say the thing that separates Phish from the other bands is that—this kind of goes along with the jam band thing—is that their reputation and fan base was built on a grass-roots community much like the Grateful Dead too, 'cause even though the Grateful Dead had the major label thing, they were selling so many concert tickets and probably millions of records too. Phish is like an extension of that 'cause they built the community just by being there. You didn't see them on MTV like many other alternative bands—at least I didn't see them!

Stephen Perkins: I think everyone who has put their foot into the pond has turned me on to be that kind of . . . to be brave enough to just go out there and be players. Starting with Gov't Mule. There is something dangerous about them, but something free about that. The Allman Brothers—I remember being younger and thinking, "How do you write a song, then go for twenty-five minutes and start playing and then come back to the tune?" Like I said, I was very fortunate to do shows with the moe. cats and the Umphrey's McGee guys, and they really care about the scene, so they really stick out as two bands that really meant something to me because they cared about it. They like talking about music, they like doing clinics, they like going to shows, and to me that was a turn to see guys so into it. I remember going on the bus with Dark Star Orchestra, and it was a lot of fun to go on their bus and see what kind of trip they were into. And I respected what they were doing. On the Jam Cruise it was Medeski, Martin and Wood, and they were amazing—really taking it to an esoteric level, just zoning out for a while—and people were still moving their bodies to it. At the Jammies, seeing everyone together backstage rubbing elbows—that was exciting to me. There are a lot of great players!

Dan Keller: For me, I saw Phish at the War Memorial in 1997, and that was one of the biggest influences for me—wanting to be able to improvise with a big crowd of people, making the vibe really big. That changed my life, and it's why I'm here right now playing music. But Bob Marley, any seventies reggae started to be an obsession for us. Listening to Lee Scratch Perry; Dylan [Savage] listened to a lot of Buddy Willard growing up.

Jake Huffman: I think musically and career-wise we are trying to forge our own path. We don't want to set the goal of "We want to be like Phish or the Flaming Lips" or to have a cult follow us. If we keep playing the music we like and are into and putting out the sound that is in our hearts and the music in our heads, then hopefully we will make our own thing for other people to look on and set their goal to us. We are just taking this a step at a time and really trying to get the most out of everything.

David Gans: Phish is like a stupid East Coast high energy thing that takes a part of the Grateful Dead and ignores the most interesting parts of the Grateful Dead. Not just lyrics but, I don't know . . . I feel like I've always kind of come down on Phish, and I try not to make really harsh public statements about them, but I've never been able to get into Phish because it seems like they are doing it on purpose—they are being shallow on purpose. Their stuff is goofy, and I would always say, yeah, they'll make you laugh, they'll make you dance, but they'll never make you cry. And they're really, really good at what they do, and I think Phish are the best post–Grateful Dead band even though they're a post–Zappa band as much as they're a post–Grateful Dead band, but

Spin Doctors, early 1990s. *(Paul La Raia)*

Bela Fleck and the Flecktones, October 31, 1991. *(Thomas G. Smith Photography)*

Members of Widespread Panic, Aquarium Rescue Unit, and Blues Traveler
at H.O.R.D.E. Tour, July 10, 1992. *(Thomas G. Smith Photography)*

Aquarium Rescue Unit in Rochester, New York, July 1993. *(Thomas G. Smith Photography)*

H.O.R.D.E. Hot Air Balloon. *(Heidi Kelso)*

Leftover Salmon in Santa Fe, New Mexico, June 24, 1997. *(Thomas G. Smith Photography)*

Widespread Panic at University of New Orleans, October 31, 1997. *(Thomas G. Smith Photography)*

Frogwings, February 14, 1999. *(Thomas G. Smith Photography)*

Gov't Mule, March 21, 1999. *(Thomas G. Smith Photography)*

Larry Campbell, Warren Haynes, and Jimmy Vivizo at Mountain Jam Festival, 2008. *(Heather Ainsworth)*

The Dead in Albany, New York, 2009. *(Heather Ainsworth)*

Donna the Buffalo at The Tralf in Buffalo, New York, 2010. *(Michelle Cormier)*

Papa Mali, Peter Conners, and Bill Kreutzmann at Mountain Jam, 2011. *(J.R. Kraus)*

Eric Krasno and George Porter, Jr., Bear Creek Festival, 2011. *(Tarver Shelton)*

Keller Williams and Alan Bartram at Magnolia Music Festival, 2011.
(Gypsyshooter-David Lee)

Hooper Faerie at Get Down Music Festival and Campout, 2011.

(*G. Milo Farineau, MiloFarineauphotography.com*)

Tim Reynolds and Dave Matthews at the Dave Matthews Caravan Festival in Atlantic City, New Jersey, June 25, 2011. *(G. Milo Farineau, MiloFarineauphotography.com)*

Phish, 2012. *(Clayton Roberts)*

Robert Randolph at Telluride Blues and Brews Festival, 2012. *(Tarver Shelton)*

Steve Kimock, 2012. *(Tarver Shelton)*

String Cheese Incident at Hangout Music Festival, 2012. *(Clayton Roberts)*

Telluride Blues and Brews Festival, 2012. *(Tarver Shelton)*

Umphreys McGee at Hangout Music Festival, 2012. *(Clayton Roberts)*

EOTO at Werk Out Music and Arts Festival, 2012. *(Mark Loveless)*

Lotus at Werk Out Music and Arts Festival, 2012. (*Mark Loveless*)

Ivan Neville with Dumpstaphunk, Mustang Music Festival,
Corolla, NC, October 2012. (*John Phillips*)

The "Pool Deck" stage on Jam Cruise 11, January 2013. JJ Grey & Mofro performing.
(*John Phillips*)

Yonder Mountain String Band with Jason Carter of the Travelin' McCourys at The Orange Peel in Asheville, North Carolina, January 25, 2013. (*Lori Sky Twohy, LSTimages.com*)

moe. at The Fillmore Charlotte, February 15, 2013. (*Brad Kuntz Photography*)

Dark Star Orchestra in Bloomington, Indiana, June 2, 2013. (*Keith Griner*)

the idea—this sort of rhetoric of their presentation, that they're going to start from one thing, go into an open-ended space, and wind up in an unknown destination—most of the bands that call themselves jam bands, that are heirs to that tradition, don't do that. They don't even try to do that, and for all I know Phish writes their set lists out ahead of time too. But I got the impression that they were truly improvising, that they are truly improvising; when they leave one place, they don't necessarily know where the next place to land is. Other bands, they just play long solos. I mean, String Cheese Incident, I never understood. I'm sorry, you guys, you're a swell bunch of people, but I never understood why so many of my Deadhead friends wound up in that dull place to have their psychedelic weekend adventures because I found so little rewarding in what they did. My wife and I were at a String Cheese show at the Greek Theatre once and, I can't remember what year, and you look around—so many of my friends looked like they had been seeing the Grateful Dead. There were so many wonderful people having a picnic, having a great time, taking their psychedelics, blah, blah, blah, and this just incredibly uninteresting music coming off that stage. Instead of a long jam where everybody's playing something interesting and they are making it interlock and building a structure, these guys were taking turns playing long-winded solos. One of them would play and then another one would play and they came coasting back down into this completely sophomoric song about "What am I going to do with my life?" or whatever, and we looked at each other and thought [shrugs] and we left. I just can't make myself love that music, and it's because the Grateful Dead set up this intensely multileveled experience where you're going to get the full range. They are going to get as dark as you can get in their songs, and they're going to get as bright and celebratory as you can get in their songs, and they're gonna go through scary parts, and then they're gonna sing a sweet ballad for you, and then there's gonna be a nice, nice rock 'n' roll tune to send you on your way. And the range of experiences that you had presented to you at a Grateful Dead concert was like all the works of Shakespeare. Steve Silverman in the intro to *The Storyteller Speaks*, a new compilation of fiction that just came out in the last couple months, Steve wrote this wonderful foreword or introduction or something, and he talked about that the Grateful Dead invented a form of storytelling without words. I think that is really just a perfect way to put it. And I remember the day I figured that out. It was at the Hollywood Bowl in 1974. I was high on acid and all my friends were high on acid, and there was this very intense thing going on in the audience. It was like they had hired jock thugs from USC to be their security or something. There was just this sort of violence in the atmosphere at the show, and I felt that very loosely at the time and I later learned that there had been stuff going on backstage as well. Bob Weir head-butted some security guy or something—I found this out years later; it kind of corroborated my sense of what had happened that day. But it was just the sense that I had that the show, the whole Grateful Dead concert, was a narrative. There was a structure, and I could not tell you the plot of that story, but that there was a narrative happening and that the show was a tale made up of these songs, and from that time on I just have this sense that these guys are storytellers, and when I describe the music that I like the best, I think of it in that sense. That's why I love Railroad Earth. And the way I describe Railroad Earth is that it's a brilliant songwriter, Todd Sheaffer, surrounded by the best storytelling musicians. And those guys all know that their job is to not show off their great wanky licks; it's to tell the story. And they do that, those guys, Railroad Earth, tells Todd's songs, and in their instrumentals there's real interaction going on between the players. Musical conversation is happening because those guys are all master storytellers without words, and that's what the Grateful Dead was giving us. When I came onboard the Grateful Dead bus in the seventies they were doing that. There would be twenty to thirty minutes without a song, without a lyric being sung, in which they were dropping tonality, they were dropping tempo, they were going into sound effects. There were these passages one of my buddies called "whale talk," and it was stuff . . . it was very, very moody and dark and quiet, and it would be, like, no sound for a few seconds, and then there would be this kind of [makes whale sound] thing, or Jerry would be playing muted stuff with the wah-wah pedal that would be at the low end of the frequency sweep, you know, and then there'd be . . . he'd open up the wah-wah pedal and there'd be [makes wah-wah sound] and, you know, there was just, like, sound effects and lyrical musical stuff—I mean lyrical in the guitar playing, not singing, you know. It was just a tremendous range of emotional content being presented as a conversation among these incredibly brilliant band of guys on stage.

Stephen Perkins: To me the music itself on record, beautiful songs, but it was when I went to the [Grateful Dead] show at two in the afternoon but the gig wasn't until 9 p.m., hanging out in the parking lot with acoustic guitars and bongos, going to different scenes, meeting people, having a community before the concert, and that put me in a great headspace. That put me in a space where anything goes and I'm open to anything and I love having the dynamics of having all those people together for one reason: to celebrate music. You see punks, you see nuns, you see hippies, you see folk musicians, you see metal guys—it's all there, and I love that feeling. Then me and [Dave] Navarro would start going to a lot of shows together, walking around with the acoustic, and I'd have my bongo and we'd go play for people. It was just all part of the scene, and as the show approached and darkness fell and maybe a nibble on a mushroom or a smoke and start getting in the mood, and it just felt like something special was going to happen. Tomorrow morning I won't be the same person. You go into the show, and people are dancing in the halls. They have speakers in the bathroom, the party is everywhere, you can't escape it—it's not just at your seat; that's great if you want to be there, but you don't have to be. Then you go in and you can't believe how quiet it is—you're talking to your buddy, saying, "They're full blast?" "No, they're dynamic. They will get loud, and then they will calm down." They cum in your face and tickle your balls! No, no, I'll take that back. They'll slap you in the face and blow in your ear! That's a Grateful Dead show! It's all a story, and in your head it all makes sense, and of course as drums and space would approach, the psychedelic experience would grow, and you think to yourself, "What could be next?" And all of a sudden the sound is coming from behind you, and it sounds like pipes are breaking, and you look up and it's just Jerry touching his guitar and Mickey banging on a pipe, and you can't believe what's happening, but you can appreciate they're out there in front of twenty thousand people enjoying themselves on their instruments and anything goes. I saw them play with Ornette Coleman—I've never seen Jerry play better. I've seen them play with Steve Winwood—I've never seen Bobby sing better. I've seen them play with Santana—I've never seen Billy play better. They would bring people onstage, and the level would just rise. Ornette Coleman came out, and Jerry was like, "Wait, man, you thought our first hour was good? Just wait till Ornette is standing next to me and we're gonna go for a ride!" And I think rock musicians and folk musicians and lovers of music were not even prepared for what the Dead was bringing them. They were bringing some hotshots onstage that we heard about from the sixties, when Bill Graham was putting on Miles Davis shows with the Airplane and the Dead. The Dead said, "We're still gonna do it. If you're around, come aboard." And I always thought that was great 'cause the Dead said to themselves, "We have great songs, great following, but what's next? Let's stretch it." And those were great experiences for me to see how a community can be formed. How rubbing against the right people can bring you to a new level, and that is really important because I am forty-four and have a wife and kid, but what turns me on is other musicians. That's what makes me want to practice. Or seeing some other hotshot or playing with a hotshot. I always thought you meet these musicians and they are so great, and they turn out to be regular guys like you and me that like to play and that's all it is—just sharing that experience. And sometimes there may be influences that are way beyond you, so sometimes you just put your sticks down and just watch and enjoy, and when I feel comfortable I'm back in. Like a conversation: if you have nothing to say, shut up for a minute. But it was really the Dead shows and that experience of before the show and watching these guys doing it onstage fearlessly, and if they drop the ball with no net, so what? They kept going. If Bobby forgot the lyrics, the crowd loved him for it. And that was a great experience for me, to see the trust between them—the audience and musician and musician, and sound man, and sound man and lighting guys. It was just a great community, and then after the show you see a hundred girls dancing and a VW bus playing KC and the Sunshine Band and the party continued, and you wonder, *Where is Billy right now? Where is Jerry right now?* It's a lot of fun to open yourself up to everybody and let them in.

Papa Mali: Absolutely, it was incredible! Me and a bunch of my friends had been looking forward to it for a long time. I was still in high school, so I had to lie to my parents and say I was spending the night with a friend. It was a great experience. A friend of mine had turned me on to the Dead about a year and a half earlier—that's when I followed them; the closest was when I first discovered them and for several years after that. I had all the records from about '68 to '76. I still listened after that, but I started on my own musical path, so I wasn't as hardcore of a fan, of any band really. I was still a fan but not going on tour because I was going on tour with my own band.

John Skehan: It seems to me, unintentionally, that a lot of the songs have fallen into two categories. Some of them come out, some straight from Todd in their form. We add some instrumentations, some color, perhaps some arrangement choices. They pretty much stay true to that genesis from the day they are recorded or set down until now. Others—just by nature of the song, be it the lyric content or vibe of the music from the beginning or outset—showcase themselves as vehicles for improvisation or stretching out on. So I don't think we take some songs randomly and say let's jam on this one tonight. There are some that in their concept both lyrically or musically are very song or songwriter oriented, and others come out saying there's a. . . . Something like "Seven Story Mountain" or "Smiling Like a Buddha" would be good examples. I think from the get-go when they started it seemed natural. It didn't feel like we were forcing it, like, okay this would be a place to jam. It was just that the lyrics set up this mood, the music sets up this mood, and it wants to take on a wider breadth through improvisation or through extended arranging.

Michael Travis: Back in the day we did as much as we could to foster it, as far as touring in a way that everyone could get on board with and always make the drives conscientious so that everyone could be able to be a part of it. It was just more of an intention to know that's what we wanted to be a part of. And using the Grateful Dead model as always a beacon . . . I was always a big proponent of improvisation knowing that that brought people together, it made people . . . not only did it make people want to come back night after night because they didn't know what was going to happen, and they'd be afraid to miss something, but I also have this feeling with improv that it's a moment when you'd hear backstories, back in the day of some guy saying, "Dude, Jerry was playing that one solo during 'Scarlet Begonias,' and I swear I told him what to play," and I believe that because when you're in a state of improv, the entire room, you reach a closer state of dropping your individual identities and becoming a single unit, where your mind is absolutely closer to a part of Jerry's mind and can influence him. That's why I was always intoxicated with the concept of improv, which is why I always tried to push it and push it so that the whole room could achieve liftoff and the audience members could absolutely be playing the instruments, and we were just kind of the conduits or the stand-ins that had done the time to learn how the fingers are supposed to work, but . . . it's not that we were feeling that exactly at any given moment, but I'm positive it was happening. So just the improv alone was enough fostering, and also the song material started to become more and more self-help oriented or personal beacon on how we can all grow community and grow ourselves. Instead of, you know, "My mom wronged me—all I wanted was just one Pepsi and she wouldn't give it to me." I was like, "No, we're all in this together," and using Robert Hunter's lyrics in that whole thing, again, as a beacon for community building.

Papa Mali: I think his [Robert Hunter's] whole thing is that he wants whoever is singing his words to be able to believe in them. And that is important. It's hard to sing someone else's words if you don't know where you are coming from.

Stephen Perkins: I'm friends with this guy Howard Cohen who works with Mickey Hart, and Howard introduced me to Steve Kimock. And Kimock started jamming with my band, Banyan. It was Kimock and Banyan. And Kimock's scene was a lot deeper in the Dead than my scene as far as the Dead guys. So Kimock sort of introduced me to that world, and the first night we played together was at the Jammys, and Mickey came up and played the cowbell and Billy played some drums with me. I felt like a hero. I could die that night—in between Billy and Mickey on "my" stage for the Jammys. It was a crazy night. That's when it all started, and then the next night there was a party somewhere deep in New York, and the Rhythm Devils were playing, so I showed up and did some bongo work, and I felt at home. I have been to over one hundred Dead shows, and now I'm with these guys playing and offering what I have to say, hoping the communication was there, and it was, and it started to grow. As far as rhythm, there is so much to happen and so many tiny little rhythms, like a cricket, or there are huge rhythms like a huge wheel, and this can all be happening inside one little band. Mickey could be playing the big rollover rhythm, and I could be playing the tiny rhythms, and Billy could be doing more finesse, and all these different rhythms are happening and we're listening, and that is without bass, guitar, keyboard, trumpet, singers. There is just a real melodic drum circle going on. To me I can get lost in that. Lost in the drum circle. I love seeing those rhythms and girls getting loose. There is something real special when you watch Billy and Mickey play. They have been together fifty years, and what they have—it's just there. I met Navarro when I was fifteen, and I'm forty-four now, and we have played together the whole time. Same thing: we don't even have to say anything; it's just there since high school marching band. That was great for me having to play with twelve other great drummers, but it made me practice! It was cool 'cause everyone was into different things, so we all showed each other different things. It is great improvising with musicians 'cause Kimock doesn't have the same record collection that I do, so we are onstage together, and what's gonna happen? I will pull from my influences over the last thirty years, and Kimock is pulling from his, and of course whatever is going on in the audience or whatever happened that day . . . if something great happened to me that day, I'm gonna put it in my drumming; if something crappy happened, that is going in too. I like to pull from the environment—that is what improvising is all about. You shouldn't go in with a plan. You should go in with what's happening at that moment, what's turning you on. Just like going out to dinner, a conversation goes, "How was your day?"—you talk about it. But with drums and guitar you don't talk; you play how you are feeling and really listen. In some drumming it's great to just be the pulse, but you have to stop listening to be the pulse. There is something great about some of the young musicians coming up and what they are pulling from. I got to pull from jazz and rock, and as I got older I got into East Indian music and African music. Mickey Hart also turned me onto some rhythms I was never aware of until Mickey brought them to my attention. So just to be involved with young musicians that are pulling from all these different influences, plus all the old stuff we had, and where their head's going and technology today, everything is coming at you. A musician growing up in New York City is gonna sound very different than a musician who grows up in Miami. You have to pull from your environment and what's going on. I'm a California boy. I think a lot of LA music is below the waist, a lot about sex, where New York music is above the neck, more about thinking. Somewhere between is improvising, using your head and your balls. It's gotta have sex appeal, sex drive—that's how we move on as a race. But then again you have to have something to think about too. It's not all about sex. I play great when I'm alone, but if I'm surrounded by girls dancing, I think I play a little better. Something happens; there is a chemical reaction as you play with great musicians. You're sitting down with Mickey Hart or Kimock, and all of a sudden you get turned on that something is gonna happen where it wouldn't happen with someone else. Even with my first jam with Kimock we didn't say hi for more than a minute. We just hit the stage, and that's where we found each other.

Perry Farrell: There are musicians that you meet—and it has gotten somewhat rare—that you meet a musician and their love of music . . . it's like they don't even need eyes because their ears are so perceptive and so in tune and they love life through listening. Not so much today. The young people don't really have that gift. I think it comes because outside stimulations that are not music now entertains them. They are looking into a video game a lot of times and, yes, music is playing behind the video game, but they are not so aware of the song. There are some musicians that are coming up—Dhani [Harrison] is such a guy. There are musicians that still exist that serve as our inspirations and our heroes—Bob [Weir] is one such fellow. Jane's Addiction is kind of in between those guys. We carry the torch because we were never really a big pop sensation; our thing was come dig our shindig, our show, and magic is gonna happen there. And that is not something you can go pick off a shelf. It's not for everyone. This is something that is a ritual and that is primitive—it's primal. It's roots, or at least it realizes it without realizing it. They like to go out and experience and participate and socialize in a musical surrounding, and although we are not a jam band per se, I think that is where we all connect and all touch. We are real musicians, and we can make the magic happen, live.

Building Fans
and Avoiding the Man

John Rider: We were always trying to innovate and be cutting edge. We were looking at technology and building our own PA system. Part of that innovation was coming up with ways to promote the band. I think we were one of the first bands—before the Internet—we had the concept of the mailing list. That bred this following of people. We had a hotline, which I don't think any other band at the time had. And all that together kept our following, and we had a way to communicate with the following, along with word of mouth. I think being innovative like that has helped us really carve out a niche and develop this following all across the country, even though we never really go across the country. The first time we went to California we did great out there; there were tons of people. Plus, the people who came to see us every Wednesday night, they would go to Providence to come see us. I think that kind of loyalty is something that has helped us persevere and made this the thing it is. Mailing lists went out on a monthly basis to everyone on it; therefore, someone from Boston would come to Rochester or vice versa. Then we had the hotline number, and everyone at the door got a card with that on it. I still get people today who pull out this dog-eared card and say, "I still have the hotline number." But I say, "Don't call it. The number now belongs to a local cop!"

Mark Mercier: Our publicity was always on the homegrown side, which I think endeared us to a lot of people—'cause we were them. We always considered our audience an intricate part of the band. They were important, and we treated them like that.

Keith Mosley: We're a bunch of regular guys with an upstart business from Colorado. We happen to be able to do what we love. And the getting together, the community thing, has always been huge for us, and continues to be. Playing Red Rocks last summer, I remember going out there, the first set in the daylight, and looking . . . I feel like I know 70 percent of the crowd personally! These are people we've been seeing and playing to. We played their wedding, they've been to our bar shows here and there, we've known them forever. And I think our shows have become a real gathering place, and I can't tell you how many people I've talked to that say, "Oh, I met my best friend at your show" or "I met my wife at your show" or "My business partner, we've been coming to your shows for years." I met my wife at one of our shows in Lake Tahoe. It's just the people that it's brought together and the community that it's created has really been bigger than anything musically we've ever done, and for me that's as amazing as any part of it. Just somehow we've become this magnet that has brought so many great people together.

Justin Carrey: We are certainly not experts on the whole social networking thing. I do know enough to know it's changed a lot from paper-handed bills to event updates. Like Facebook and

Myspace—the whole bit. It's changed for the better. The music business is changing so rapidly, but it gives bands like us an opportunity to sit in the driver's seat. We don't have to worry about if we can afford to print out ten thousand flyers; the Internet has made reaching out free.

Jason Ott: One of the things that worked for us is having such a tight family, and being so supportive, they took on jobs. My mom is the "merch mom"—always behind the merchandise tables. My dad records the shows and puts them up for free. His [Jake Huffman] mom became the manager; it just happened like that. It has worked for us so far. We have had record label offers, but to us this just makes sense.

George Porter Jr. [interview from *Gonola.com*]: Advice is a dime a dozen these days. If there is any advice to be had: if you're going to get into this business to earn money, learn the business. If you just want to get into this business just to have fun and enjoy playing, I still say learn the business side. Doing it just to enjoy what you're doing, you may start doing something that's really good. Somebody is going to see that. They may want to start doing things. Last thing is, don't sign no piece of paper you don't understand, even when you've got a lawyer telling you, "Oh yeah, this is okay." I'm saying this because I'm going through that shit right now. I'm fighting for my life. I'm sixty-two years old. The troubles I'm having at sixty-two is the shit I'm supposed to be having at twenty-six. I've had similar things like this before, but it never got to where it is now. At sixty-two years old I'm supposed to be really enjoying what I'm doing, not figuring out how I'm going to save my home or lose my vehicles—stuff like that—because of some piece of paper that lied from the get-go, from the start. It was wrong from the start. People that told me that it was good didn't know what they were talking about. I don't write contracts. You've got to trust somebody to read a contract to you, to tell you what the here and there mean. If that person you choose to read the contract don't have a clue, they just screwed you. My advice, don't sign no paper. Managers come and go. I think, man, your life is much better without one.

Michael Travis: Probably the primary thing I noticed is how many bands back in the nineties got crushed. Like Jason Hann, a percussionist, he had a band called Zoo People that absolutely just got crushed and destroyed by a shitty record deal, with a monster, maybe it was Columbia or Atlantic or something. Just "We're going to release the album in six months," and, "Oh, don't worry," and then after a while they would be like, "We are just going to put it on the back burner for a minute until . . . " and you know, they were waiting for the album to release before they toured, and it just went [makes raspberry noise], and I think that happened a lot. And since we foresaw that problem before it would happen, and just releasing our own albums we had total autonomy in that way. I think that's the main thing that could have damaged our longevity and didn't. Other things are pretty standard: having our own merch company, having our own ticketing company and our own travel agency, and that stuff. But getting our own record company just made it. So there was never even a thought, and just watching another band that was just killin' and got crushed by record company stuff—it happens all the time.

Chuck Garvey: We had one guy who was excited about us, but I don't think the label really caught on to it. Or we didn't perform to Sony's expectations.

Rob Derhak: Basically they had a formula where you do things *this* way, and if it works out, everyone is happy, and if not, you just go on your way. And we just didn't write a "radio hit."

Marco Benevento: We had some experience with some smaller labels. Joe Russo and I have the Benevento/Russo Duo, and we put out some records on Ropeadope, and I was a guest on some other friends' records, and around that time record labels were starting to transition to more electronic sales from actual CD sales. Labels in general around that time, around 2004, were dealing with the transition and possibly losing staff and shrinking. It was always in the back of my mind that we should do that—we put in all our money and we get it all back, we won't have to deal with paying the label. Joe and I, even back when we were heavily touring, we started our own label, so it started a little before the Royal Potato Family even started. We didn't really have our heads in it, though; our manager was taking care of things. So it started around that time. Then Joe and I took a bit of a break, and then my own band started touring a little more. Then I put out an album with Hyena, which is the last record label that I worked with before I started with the Royal Potato Family. So I put out *Invisible Baby* on Hyena, and I was working with Kevin Calabro, my manger, and that is really when I was like, "Okay, next record I have to put this out on my own because I see where all the money is going, I see what's happening, and a lot of things don't make sense to me." I feel like if we have a team, if I work closely with my manager and we really put our heads together . . . luckily my manager is a publicist, so he knew that side of things. So seeing where the money goes and how things go—if money comes in, sometimes half the money or more goes to the label before you see any of it. Granted, the label does put in a lot of money and time for publicity and do a lot of things for you. This way, doing it myself, I have noticed, makes you work that much harder to try and get your money back. Kevin Calabro was a big help with that, and now I see what's really going on and how a record is really made and promoted and how much it really costs to do it well. I have been so busy touring and working that I don't do much of the day-to-day stuff. Kevin does the majority of it, and it really is a lot of work. We have a lot of our friends on our label along with some new bands I haven't heard of. We actually now need more people working for us; it is really starting to grow!

Eric Krasno: I guess the cool thing about that time [1990s] is that it was leading up to the height of the record industry, so one thing that a lot of bands from that time know is that you could go out and be a touring band and grow as a band and gain an audience and sell your music, and that is something that we know.

Tim Bluhm: Well, "Third Floor Story" is pretty autobiographical. It's easy to write a song like that in this business. We have had a lot of challenges, but the good thing about it is we've never given up. We had a brush with the real music industry, and it did a lot of good for us, and then we sort of got booted out of it, and I was ultimately looking back on it now. It was a great thing for us 'cause we learned how to survive with our own money and make our own money, not spending more than we make, and that's how we run our band. When everything is collapsing in the music industry and no one is selling records, it doesn't matter to us at all. I don't think anyone would brag about our business model necessarily, but we have made a living at it the eighteen to twenty years our band has been together. We are very grateful for that. We are working hard all the time.

Michael Kang: None of the industry models really applied to us as much, just because when we first started out we were more into just playing for fun and just going to ski towns and skiing. It was more of a lifestyle choice for us. We were still living in the ski towns in the winter, wanting to ski at lunch. We had this rec-reationally driven lifestyle for the first couple years of the band. It wasn't just about playing music. We were playing music, but we wanted to have as much fun as possible too. We weren't even traveling to the cities. That wasn't even part of the whole scheme.

Perry Farrell: I don't know what the industry is going to do next, but I know what we are going to do next, and that is going to go back and record for the familiarity. I like the fact that people know our songs when we arrive. But I'm building an entirely new con-cept for experiencing live music. Our whole world was based on being on the road, being on a bus—it's where I feel most comfort-able, where I am most healthy. When I'm not I feel sick. So part of it is for self-preservation. It keeps me young, I enjoy it, it is helpful to me. This morning I found a 1972 video documentary about the Grateful Dead to fill in my wife about them and to explain to her their legend, to really know them more. I was telling her how the music doesn't attack you; it just lets you be. It's more just a social environment. This particular documentary took place in Oregon, and Bill [Graham] had these hippies building the stands out of logs and wood, and seats using handsaws. It was from scratch. People just want to have a concert. That's why I say those days are not gonna happen again. These people were really united, doing it all as a group. Today you have parking that they will tax you for, tickets, some better than others, screwed-in seats. Jane's Addic-tion tries hard to stay out of amphitheaters for that very reason. It almost killed Lollapalooza.

I need a little kinetic energy in the GA. I need people to be able to dance and groove. I don't want the restriction of seats, and I don't like the aristocracy of "I have more money than you, so I can get a better view."

Jon Guttwillig [interview from the *Dartmouth Independent*]:
There's still a culture around the music. And people have gotten
better at providing a culture. I mean, look at Woodstock 1999, the
thirty-year anniversary. It was like Limp Bizkit and all of the day's
big pop bands, and it was a disaster. It was a disaster because the
people who did the festival didn't understand how to create the
event.

And now you look at Bonnaroo, which is as big as Woodstock—maybe not as big as the original, but as big as the thirtieth
anniversary—and a couple others that are that big, and you look
at the huge sporting events. You have this world where instead
of selling music, you're selling culture to some degree. That's
not really my job, but it is a part of what you want to do. It's part
of reaching your customer on a good level, it's part of reaching
your fans, it's part of connecting with your audience. You want to
connect with them. You want them to not only take home, "Hey,
that was a great party, I met a cool girl, blah blah blah." You want
them to have a little moment of inspiration in there. Maybe they
go home and have a little realization or something. You can't force
the realization; you just have to be like, "Hey, here's the material,
here's this kind of world, we're trying to make it as nice as possible for you."

And I think, generally, the club owners, the different bands,
the management companies, the concert throwers around the
country—they're all pretty hip to this idea. Whereas in 1995, not
so hip. It was more about treating your club like it was the Berlin
Wall, treating your fans like they're lucky to be there and you can
throw them out at any second. Now it's different. You try to embrace the culture and you try to add to it. You try to contribute to
it in a positive way, and you try to connect with your audience. I
think everyone pretty much agrees that's the way to do it.

John Bell [**interview from *Swampland***]: Phil Walden [of Capricorn Records] really had other plans and bands, but we were the flagship group. Honestly, we were already set in our ways as far as being a band and not a bunch of poseurs or a formula for the music industry. So along those lines I think we were a disappointment because we'd been doing our bit for so long we weren't easily remolded. I think that rubbed Phil the wrong way sometimes. We had some interesting conversations. It was an old-style record contract. CDs were just coming out, and the record industry hadn't changed yet. We were looking at a guarantee of a lot of money for the next eight to ten years. That was a great dose of backstop for you as a musician. We were making like $60 a week each after we incorporated the band. The next raise was like $87 or something. Then, you know . . . the economy is more of a whopper than industry or technology. When we went through that recession in the early nineties it was the same thing. Bands that relied on their hair or the light show fell by the wayside. We were still out there just playing. Whether it's times of escape or celebration, people will want to go out and watch a band or see a comedian as long as they're not being lied to. Folks want something to immerse themselves into. We just kept on doing what we do. Now the whole thing is happening again. Folks are not as inclined to sign up and pay to travel the whole spring tour, but that's cool, because you're playing to a decidedly different audience every night. Then you see these same bands say they're canceling tours because of personal reasons, but they just can't sell tickets.

David Gans: Well, yeah, the Grateful Dead pioneered that, quite by accident—they became a tribal thing. And that wound up—over the last twenty years or so—that became a viable economic model. The Grateful Dead modeled it by accident, Phish copied it on purpose, and then in the wake of those two, all these other bands developed. I was friends with moe., wonderful bunch of guys and another sort of band that had to escape the jam band rubric because they're not that. I think of them as a guitar god band. And I think they are the best goddamn guitar god band out there. But they very consciously built their audience the same way: with grassroots marketing, encouraging tape trading, e-mail lists. They built a tribe in the modern way, quite consciously, and also exist and thrive completely outside the mainstream, as near as I can tell. They play in the Bay Area at least once a year, and I think they do really well. They host their own festivals, and they make enough money to put their kids through college and everything else without bothering with the mainstream music business, and they did that by seeing how the Grateful Dead did it and choosing the parts that were worth doing and doing it. Some other bands, same thing: they can look at the Grateful Dead as a model of how to market, as a tribal model of how to market music, and if you can deliver the goods and attract an audience and build a tribe, then you can succeed. The Grateful Dead tried to make hit records and stuff, and they just failed for the most part and instead wound up becoming a sustainable touring band. So they never had the rise-and-fall thing that a band would have that sold a lot of records and wound up imitating themselves in casinos into their fifties and sixties. The Grateful Dead instead got to continue evolving, although there was a certain stultifying thing as well, just due to age—the excesses of adoration they had was also a terrible demotivator for innovation. But as long as they could keep themselves interested, other people would stay interested in what they were doing. And that is a model that all the rest of us should be so lucky to be able to follow.

If the music is good, that's the thing—it's always in the grooves. There's only so much you can do with hype. There's a certain amount of astroturfing that you can do by . . . that's phony grass-roots marketing. It came out of the political world. The whole Tea Party thing is a massive astroturfing thing, incredibly well funded by vicious right-wing motherfuckers, to fool idiots into pretending that they thought it up themselves and that they hate the government. Dick Armey is the king of the goddamn Tea Party—outsider, my ass! So there have been bands—and I don't want to get into specifics because it's just badmouthing—but there have been bands that had backing of usually a grower—people with money to spare and good taste in music—who would underwrite them so they could go play festivals and play gigs for nothing, take every shit gig and go out and build an audience. And they would leaflet—you know, they did all that stuff you do. They would poster towns and hire people to be their fans basically, to promote them and create a social scene around the band, and then that's how the band would rise up and build an audience and demonstrate. 'cause there's this huge catch-22 in the music business: you can't get a booking agent until you can demonstrate a draw, and you can't get good gigs to build a draw until you've got somebody to help you get 'em. So it's really, really hard to break up off the ground floor, and furthermore these days the ceiling has come way, way down. People don't sell ten million records anymore, very few people do. If you're lucky, you can top the charts and be a huge smashing success and maybe sell half a million units because people just aren't buying music.

So the tribal model is the one that works, and now, since you've given away so much of the music for free, to market yourself, you're making your money on tickets sales and merchandise, and the CD becomes just another piece of merch on the table, next to the stickers and the T-shirts, and you're probably making more money on the T-shirts. A guy like me, who has nothing but his music, I can't afford to carry T-shirts. I can't pay to have them designed and printed; I don't have a guy to schlep 'em around. I have no mechanism to sell that shit at shows. I have a couple of little things of my CDs that I bring with me, and I'll sit at the table after the show and sign and sell CDs, and that's how I sell 80 percent of my music, how everybody sells 80 percent of their music. As much the artifact and the contact and the autograph than it is in the grooves itself. People came to the show, they enjoyed what they heard, and they want to take something home. I'd probably sell as many T-shirts as CDs, and I should, because T-shirts are advertising. If I had people walking around with a T-shirt with my mug on it, I'd probably be more successful. That's an investment I haven't been able to make. But that tribal thing is the model now, and that emanated directly from the Grateful Dead, who, by the way, did not really invent it. They got it from the bluegrass and country western world. I remember going to see Dolly Parton at the Flint Center in Santa Clara once, and after the show she stood in the door of her bus and signed autographs until every single person had got what they wanted from her and was gone. And that's how you did business in that world. At the same time, the rock 'n' roll world was full of mysterious characters that you never saw except when they were on stage, and their whole thing was inaccessibility. Bluegrass: Jerry Garcia, Sandy Rothman, drove across the country in that Corvair in 1964 with that tape recorder in the backseat to go to bluegrass festivals and hope for a chance to pick with Bill Monroe and record Jim and Jessie [McReynolds] and to get near the artists, and in that world, in that tradition, there would be campfire jams. And you'd meet other musicians of your generation and you'd meet other musicians of the previous generation and you'd actually get to hang out with your heroes, 'cause that's how that world worked. The Grateful Dead came up as a neighborhood band in the Haight with all these other great neighborhood bands; then they got this huge amount of world attention, some of them went on into the mainstream music business, like Jefferson Airplane, sold billions of records, became that kind of degenerate superstar kind of thing. The Grateful Dead had to work a little harder because they weren't selling records; they had to grind out the gigs. They formed their bond with their audience by repeating high-quality engagement without selling records. This tribe formed around them, and as all the rest of that counterculture hippie shit evaporated, they wound up keeping what was left of it stuck to them and wound up getting credit for all of it because they were the last surviving avatars of it. You read Peter Coyote and other clear-headed accounts of that time, you realize that there was so much else going on, and Jerry would have been the first to acknowledge that; Jerry didn't need any of that credit laid on him. The Grateful Dead wound up getting the credit and the blame for huge amounts of it because they were the last surviving hippie band, and Jerry wasn't even a hippie. Jerry was a Beat.

Jeff Lloyd: We do have a record label. They're a South Florida label, we're their only band, and it's been an awesome opportunity for us because they have allowed us to really go after a lot of those things we've always wanted to accomplish. They have given us the freedom to attempt some things that, if we were on our own, maybe we couldn't have. They support us tremendously. We owe a lot of what we've done in the past couple years to them.

Justin Carrey: We record every one of our shows, and those are available online—I think it's livedownloads.com. But as far as recording albums, we are always working on recording our songs in the studio, and we would probably have a release for something we were serious about, but it would be available online for sure. And I'm sure if you dug hard enough, you could find it online for free. I'm not necessarily endorsing that, but it happens; it comes with the territory. We are talking about how the music industry has changed, so you have to expect that every ten records that people are hearing, nine of them were free.

Andrew Altman: I think that is part of the nature of being a band that survives so much on touring. In this genre, in this scene that we live in, it—whatever you want to call it—that's the bulk of your survival. The people who are supporting you are consuming your show, and they want to see something different every time. It kind of evolves out of that expectation. The fans that enjoy this type of music aren't going to let you get away with playing the same song the same way night after night. People who want to see that kind of show are going to go see more polished pop acts or things like that, where they just want to see the song executed like the record. Fans that live in our world expect more. We use that as motivation to find ways to stretch out, to stretch out the songs.

Tara Nevins: Well, the way it started, though, was that it was literally two people. These two fans would come to see us, and it was like, "Okay, well, I'm going to the show in Cincinnati—let's meet behind the soundboard." And these two people would meet behind the soundboard and go, "Here we are." And it grew from there. And now it's this self-perpetuated, self-contained thing. But we had nothing to do with organizing it. You can just be a fan and not think about the Herd at all. But there are many layers. There is a core of the Herd that we know, and they have become friends. Then there is the next ring out. And it goes like this. And then there are just people who are fans. But it's all the Herd. It's the gathering. They do some awesome things. They come to many of our shows. They travel on whole tours with us. They have something called the Herd charity, in which they will auction off something at a show, something memorable, something of Jeb's or mine, an old something of the band's—who knows what. And whatever money they raise they will pick a local charity of the town we're in. Say right now we're in Rochester, and if they did it tonight, they might give it to the women's shelter of Rochester. And so, you know, they'll show up at places and bring us food and liquor and . . . this shirt right here! A lot of them have become really great friends and great people. It's just a really positive movement.

Jeb Puryear: This nine-year-old girl drew this buffalo, and it was one of our first posters and we made it into a T-shirt. And Richie, who is a very funny fellow, coined the phrase, "Herd of 'em?" And then it got written across the back of it. So then people started calling themselves the Herd.

Al Schnier: The fact that we have these people who come and see us fifty, seventy-five, one hundred times. . . . They have a name for seeing us seventy-six times—they call it their Strazza Line, because we had our drummer, Mike Strazza, who only played seventy-six shows with us. So if you see the band seventy-six times, then you hit your Strazza. If you see the band more than that, then you've effectively been to more moe. shows than one of the drummers in the band.

Trey Anastasio [interview from *Gladiel.com*]: It's the experience at the concerts. There's a real feeling between us. I don't feel like I'm performing *at* the audience. It's like a party. Or it's like some night in high school, where you blew off some plans, and instead you and your friends stay out all night. You went to the lake and watched the sun rise. It was a spontaneous bonding experience that you remember all your life. That's how I feel at a show when everything goes right. It's much more powerful than a planned-out show. When people have that experience, they're hooked.

Joe Russo: Absolutely, it feels like every single gig I did leading up to this [playing with Furthur], it was like this slum dog millionaire thing, where once I got here I could go back and pick the moment out where I was playing with Chris Harford and learning how to play behind a singer, and play slow and quiet playing with Fat Mama, and listening to Zeppelin as a kid. It is such a cool gig, especially now that we are a band and the trust level is there. It's just so cool to have the opportunity to access all of that on a given night and it works. Like Bob and Phil are so cool; they are not so precious with what has been done before. The idea of whatever makes music—that is the thing that always sticks out for me with those guys. They are ready to access anything. . . . For sure the fans are very forgiving too 'cause they know you are trying to go for something that isn't just right there—it's gonna take some effort. The fans give us the opportunity to experiment and not worry because they are a listening, forgiving, involved fan base.

Joel Cummins: That is the truth. Rodney Dangerfield was at one of our first shows at the club where we were playing. I'm sure people were buying him drinks, so he was enjoying himself that night, and depending on who you ask, it was either him not speaking clearly or a faulty microphone cable, but the original name of the band, "Hubert Humphrey's Traveling Band featuring Flabby McGee," kind of came out as Umphrey's McGee. So we just ran with it from there. We have signed some nice portraits that people have drawn of Rodney Dangerfield and our name in there. So R.I.P Rodney, but your legend will live on forever, and we will carry the torch for you.

Stephen Perkins: I got to meet some great guys—Umphrey's McGee and the moe. cats and String Cheese. This was five or six years ago, but they were into it. They were like, "We're not gonna stop. We're gonna go from here to Timbuktu and play for these people!" It's great to see how the scene has grown and how these younger musicians are hungry to play in front of people and improvise and show off a little and they want it. I went on a Jam Cruise that was kind of fun. It was with Banyan. Flaming Lips were there, which was very crazy to see those freaks walking around a cruise ship for three days. There were so many great bands. It was an experience to not only watch people play all the time but to just kick it in the bar and talk to people about music. Everyone was there for the music.

Joel Cummins: Definitely, we are great friends with the guys in moe. from Upstate New York. We do Summer Camp with them every year. The guys in Yonder Mountain String Band have become great friends of ours. We just did a show with them in the Saranac Brewery in Utica. The guys in the Disco Biscuits we do a festival with, and Sound Tribe Sector 9 are great friends as well—we do the holidays and Caribbean events with them, there are so many. When you do the festival circuit, it feels like you see these people every summer. It's kind of like a family reunion. It's really introduced us to so many great musicians too. We have met and performed with Huey Lewis, Mavis Staples, Josh Redman, Buddy Guy, Stanley Jordan—we even had the Chicago Mass Choir come sing with us. This is another Chicago thing, the gospel sound that's there. They are performing with us again at our Thanksgiving shows. It's a cool thing to cross-pollinate and become friends with the people I just mentioned. It's everything from, like, blues, bluegrass, live electronica to house, and all these different styles of music. We are in a very fortunate position where we can fit in with a lot of different things. We played at Telluride Blues and Brews Festival as well, or we play on Jam Cruise. We are lucky that we can morph for what it is we feel we need to gear towards the audience.

Reid Genaur: Strangefolk performed in Vermont, and Assembly of Dust was a little less centralized, but more or less New Hampshire is where the first seeds were sown for Assembly of Dust. You tend to have the strongest pulse where you live, but what's always been cool with both bands is to go across country and show up in California or Denver or Atlanta, and you have an audience that's playing back to you your own songs and vibe. It's cool to see how ideas and cultures spread beyond the spawning ground, and musically it's cool 'cause you're like, "I hatched this idea in my bedroom, and here I am three thousand miles away with total strangers playing it back to me." It's a big piece of the creative feedback loop; the life that a song or band or repertoire of music takes on, it's beyond you.

Rob Koritz: There have been a lot of constants over the years, but I think as time has gone on . . . when we first started it was a lot of older Deadheads coming to check it out. As time has gone on I've noticed we've been able to cater to a slightly younger crowd. But more importantly than their age was whether they got to see the Dead or not. I think over the years we are getting a lot more people that didn't get to see the Dead, and maybe we are giving them a little bit of a taste of what it might have been like—hearing music played in its truest form. I don't think we have lost the older people; I think we have gained the younger people.

It didn't used to be that important to me when I first joined the band. What was important to me was the people who had seen the Dead. If they came and saw us and came back 'cause they liked what we were doing, that's what validated what we were doing, in my mind. As time has gone on I've realized that's great, but my perspective has changed. It is equally important to turn on people who never got to see this music and keep it alive for their kids. So my perspective on what's important has changed—as to who we are catering to—over the years.

Dino English: I would agree, but now, later, it's almost as though those fans we turned on are still seeing us but are older and we're old. Everyone is just older. But hopefully we can continue to turn on a new generation, and that's what it's about for us. We are trying to keep this music alive, and there is only one way to do that—to turn on younger kids.

Rob Eaton: The Grateful Dead's world was vastly different from others. When you went to a Dead show, at the door you would check your sexual preferences, your political orientation, the color of your skin—none of that meant anything once you were inside. Everyone was equal, everyone was the same, and everyone was there for the same reason, which was the music. That changed later when it got really big. I think a lot of people were there for the drugs and the drug scene, but back in the seventies, once the show started there was nobody outside. Everyone was there for the show. I think what we have in the beauty of the people that come to see us is that they're there for the music. We are not the Grateful Dead. We don't want to be the Grateful Dead. But we love this music, and the people who come to see us love the music as well, and they don't care who is playing it—they just love the music and they teach the other generations. There is at least three generations of people represented a night, so the younger kids learn about the scene, about the peaceful nature, and what it was when it started. But it's not a political nature. The Grateful Dead were very clear back in the sixties that their PA systems and their microphones and speakers were for music, not political speeches or Vietnam end-the-war rallies. I think for us and the scene we have, there is no politics. It's just a small part of the best part of what the Dead scene was. The music is too good to die away. It's timeless.

Papa Mali: I think the Dead were the first band to develop a sense of community that exceeded regional borders. People, fans would follow them from city to city, state to state. People would go on tour with the Dead. People do that with the festival scene nowadays. It's really obvious that the kids who come to these festivals, they want to experience what they didn't get to experience by going on a Dead tour, and they are getting that in a lot of ways. The bands that came up in the jam band scene have definitely used the Dead as an anchor.

Bill Kreutzmann: I think we're definitely some of the reason, but not the only reason. I think it was gonna happen anyway, and we were just caught up on the wave like everyone else, even though we were some of the first. . . . In my heart, even though in the old days I wasn't as close physically, I was just as close. But now that you are close with the people and see their faces and how they are reacting, it is a great reward. Talking to your fans, people come up to you and say, "You changed my life." It's like, my god, that is quite the compliment. I'm always amazed. I never take that for granted. To tell you the truth I always held the audience in a higher esteem than [I held] the band. I think they are more important because without the audience loving us the way they did, we wouldn't be able to play the way we did.

Alan Evans: I think one big thing that kind of came out of the sixties was, people went to see live music, and it was a different era of music—you were connected to people all over the world by music not by the . . . Internet. It was a huge pivotal movement in history, and I think a part of that were these communal gatherings, coming together and showing support, and that has carried on throughout, this communal gathering of people. My dad was big into jazz and classical music, and my older brother listened to reggae and psychedelic sixties music, and we had all the music we grew up on, which was Van Halen, the Police, and it was still. . . . You talk about the megabands—that's what we grew up on, people listening to the album, you knew the album, and you went to the concerts and that is how you met people and really connected—and that is the greatest thing. People really support us and support the artists' lives. It's almost like seeing a novelist write a new chapter and then read it to you, instead of reading the same thing over and over again.

Justin Carrey: I'm really grateful to do what I do in the first place, so I really just like to make friends with the people at our shows because I appreciate them coming. I like the opportunity to meet everyone I can. We are very fortunate to have the people who come; I personally think the best way to keep in contact with them is to literally be there for them, just be a friend.

Jeff Lloyd: The thing that Justin [Carrey] is being so modest about too is that he doesn't ever put his bass guitar down when it comes to connecting with the audience. We all try to do our best. We Facebook, we meet people 'cause we want to, but really the best way to connect is to work on what we do: practice, and make sure we deliver every time we get out there.

Al Schnier [interview from *Headcount*]: If I ever doubt the validity of what we do—because you know every now and then it starts to seem silly that I play guitar for a living, it seems like I ought to be doing something more important with my life somehow when I look at the big picture. When I spend time with these people who, and it's not just because they come to our shows and take something away from the music—I mean it's great that people care so much about our music—but the thing that I really love is the fact that so many friendships have formed because of this central point that is our shows. There have been marriages and babies and these extended families, and that's the part of it that I really love. We're still so close with so many of these people. At the end of the show every night, when we do our encores, I'll read these announcements where people have seen us 75 or 150 times. It's so humbling that there's that kind of atmosphere there, and so much of it has to do with their friendships and being such a great social outlet for fans.

Trey Anastasio [interview from *The Believer*]: Today what I do is—I do this every night we play—I have a little quiet moment where I picture some guy having a fight with his girlfriend, getting into his car—the battery's dead—then he gets to the parking lot and it's full. Meets up with his friends. Comes into the show. I try to picture this one person having their own experience, and I picture them way in the back of the room. And I try to remember how insignificant my experience is, and how people's experiences with music are their own thing. We put it out there, and if it's of service to someone, great, but I try to get away from the idea that it's even starting from us. And when you do that listening-exercise stuff, which I actually get into a moment where I'm only listening, I find that the music gets so much . . . beyond us. And I can tell that from the reaction I hear from the audience. It always feels more resonant if I can get my hands off it. If all four of us were here, they'd all be saying the same thing. It's great as long as you listen to anybody but yourself. Anything but yourself.

Mickey Hart: Music has to serve the community or else the music dies. And the community needs its music—it goes both ways. In the case of the Grateful Dead, it went to a whole other level; the community had equity in the music: "Without them there would be no us!" It became a card-carrying army. They all wanted to hear the sound. I have always been thankful to have an audience that was that committed to us and the music. So you go out there and lay it on the line every night with everything you have. I will go out and do it as long as I can.

People needed to feel themselves. We were just a soundtrack to it all. We'd just come out to the park: everybody be free and loose, do what you want—just be with the music *in* the music. It's a natural extension of it. When we stopped touring there was a need . . . by that time . . . music is very much like a narcotic: I need it; without music I'd die! I would say it's very much like an opiate. It's very powerful; it can make you do things. Some people have to have it. It's part of your DNA. It makes you human and defines you. It makes you think and feel, it gives you hope, and it just happens to make us feel good. I definitely think it's a medicine not only physiologically but for the spirit.

Feelin' Festy

Dean Budnick: While the nature of Bonnaroo has shifted somewhat over the years, the first one, which featured Widespread Panic, Trey Anastasio, Phil Lesh and Friends with Bob Weir, the String Cheese Incident, moe., the Keller Williams Incident, the Disco Biscuits, Galactic, North Mississippi Allstars, Robert Randolph and the Family Band, and others, sold out in a matter of weeks without any traditional advertising (although we did run an online countdown ad campaign on Jambands.com which I created: "What is Bonnaroo, find out in XX days.") A sense of community swiftly coalesced at that first Bonnaroo, wrought from encounters with thousands of fellow travelers who had similarly stepped up and bought their tickets months in advance, anticipating a momentous event. It was all quite tangible. I am the founding editor of the festival's official free daily newspaper, the *Bonnaroo Beacon*, which publishes four editions every year, and while each Bonnaroo evokes memories and boasts highlights, none can touch the ineffable vibe of 2002.

In many respects Bonnaroo was the logical culmination of Wetlands, H.O.R.D.E., and the Phish events dosed liberally with the flavors of European festivals like Glastonbury and Reading.

James Searl: Yeah, we were playing every week at this place in Rochester—it was how we started our career for a while. Then Bonnaroo was happening in 2004 or 2005, and we really wanted to go. It was a good lineup, and we were like, "How are we going to miss this?" And we weren't booked to be there, and we were gonna have to miss our weekly gig we've done for two years to go. We said, "We can't go to this festival and see all these bands without playing." So we brought a generator and all this equipment down there in this $400 van we bought the day before and spray-painted it green. We got on the road, drove all night. It was a crazy experience—we popped two tires in Tennessee, got to the festival, and they ended up parking us in the most faraway campsite you could have been in. I just saw our whole plan closing in before our eyes. Our buddy "G," who we consider the mayor of the festivals— everywhere he goes he sets up shop and he is the vibe, people really identify with that; if you've been to a festival in the Northeast in the past fifteen years, you would recognize him. He came with a flatbed truck and a golf cart and said, "We're picking up this operation and moving it." So he moved it the next day to right in the middle of Shakedown Street. He introduced us to some vendors named Sunweaver, who were from New Hampshire. They had a complete sound system powered only off solar power. They were like, "Yeah, you can play here" and with their sound system, so we rocked out. We played like three nights in a row at Bonnaroo, more music than anyone at Bonnaroo that whole weekend. We did eight-hour sets from, like, midnight till eight in the morning. So we came back every year and started getting free tickets from the vendors, and the people in Sunweaver became some of our best friends and family. We started doing it at other festivals with them, and it was a way we could go and do what we wanted to do as kids at festivals and see all these bands we loved and inspired us and still not miss a gig. We were always down in the trenches with the people—it was dusty and dirty and hot, not sleeping for days on end 'cause it was so hot—then we'd play all through the night. That is definitely where the guerilla part of our name came from.

John Rider: That was another late-night thing. This guy Rick and I decided to have a camping festival in the town we lived in. So there was a stage made of plywood that shook. It was on somebody's farm, and people brought tents and pitched them in the woods, and we played all night. Then those went away, but they were so fun we wanted to do something similar, so one year we did one up at Granby. Then the guys up in Maine called up and asked if we wanted to do a show with them and it would be a camping festival. So we had Camp Creek II the same year in September, Labor Day. We used to set up in a hay barn, which is a half-barn used for hay storage, but they would put cows in there. We would play there, and when people danced, the manure dust would cover everything. We would have to hose our speakers off every year at the end. One year a guy ran his motorcycle into the crowd and right up to the front of the stage.

Jeb Puryear: Grassroots Festival was based on us loving to go to festivals and being a part of the old-time festivals, and there were a couple of festivals that we really liked. Croton on the Hudson was Pete Seeger's deal. And then another festival that we really liked was the Cajun Bluegrass Festival out in Rhode Island. They had a nice dance crowd, and it was late at night. They had a nice party atmosphere that we really liked.

It was very similar to the old-time party atmosphere, which is actually quite intense and very heavy partying. And so it's kind of a conglomeration. And the Hudson River Revival also had a lot of international music—lots of African bands and this and that. So between all of that conglomeration, between that and the old-time festivals that we liked, those two kind of pieced together what we thought would be great. Also, since we had come and were playing old-time music, we kept going to festivals. Now that we're playing in this band that was basically sort of a rock band, we still wanted to go to festivals, and like Tara was saying earlier, the festivals weren't as wide as a genre. It used to be the bluegrass festival or the old-time festival or this or that. So putting that on allowed us to play a festival that we really liked and were a part of. So we are lucky that festivals widened out their acceptance to allow our band and us to be a part of it, because it really feels like home to us.

Tim Bluhm: Well, Big Sur is a protected community. There is a lot of tourism, but the locals are pretty insular. You can't just go there and have a festival; it doesn't work like that. It's a small community, and they are very protective of their privacy and the way things happen, which is one of the things that make it so cool. Brit is a local promoter who I think grew up there. We hit it off, and we've always wanted to have our own festival, and we figured Brit was into it. So we started small at the Henry Miller Library in 2009, then we moved to a campground not far away that was larger. Mother Hips Family Hipnic is sort of our answer to a lot of these bigger festivals that seem a little more industrial. They are spending more money, it's usually hot and sweaty and dusty, and they are great, impressive festivals, but ours is everything these ones are not: it's small, the weather is cool, there is no chain-linked fence in the front. It's very family oriented; the music is over by 11 p.m. Everything is just a lot more manageable. You can pretty much talk to everyone that is there.

Rob Derhak: The whole idea of having a festival where people could camp and come to the show and have a fun party weekend was basically how it all [moe.down] started for us. I think the H.O.R.D.E. came out of a couple shows that those bands had all done together the summer previous to that at the Arrowhead Ranch. I guess it was ARU and Spin Doctors and Phish and Blues Traveler, and people were camping there and having a good time, so I think that sort of planted the seed that it would be nice for us to do that when we could. We started to come up with something like moe.down before there even was a moe.down. We were gonna call it the Brain Festival or something like that. That was back when we lived in Albany. When the logistics fell through and promoters fell through, it just didn't happen. After maybe two or three years the idea came up again—we still hadn't given up on the idea—and we found someone who was willing to do it. It's a natural fit for jam band music: camping, beer, music, whatever else. So we just went for it.

Al Schnier: When we started moe.down we were like the only one, we were the only band-driven festival at the time. There weren't that many festivals, period. Bonnaroo hadn't even started yet when we started moe.down. Tim Walther had just started doing festivals, but he didn't have All Good running at that time. Ekoostik Hookah had their festival and High Sierra was going, but there wasn't the myriad of festivals that we have going on, where there's several festivals every weekend all summer long. There's a huge festival scene in the summertime in the United States now—more like Europe used to be—and that's what we have in the US now, as opposed to the shed tours that we used to have, those amphitheater tours that bands used to do in the eighties and nineties. Now it's more like festival tour. You go out, and there's festivals every weekend or several festivals every weekend depending on the region, depending where in the country you are. It's kinda cool!

Keller Williams: Telluride Bluegrass Festival is one of my favorites, and High Sierra is the Cali vibe you get nowhere else—that was one of my first festivals. I don't get to play there as much as I'd like; I would love to be a regular on that festival. This festival has been very good to me too, Gathering of the Vibes. I played at this festival at two sites, one was Mariaville, I think, and the past five years it has been this one. All Good is another one that has been great to me. There are so many good ones: Live Oak in Florida, Dell Fest in Maryland; Bumbershoot in Seattle is really cool. Summerfest in Milwaukee is really cool; it's like an amusement park for concerts. It's, like, a two-week festival in downtown Milwaukee. It's so big they get, like, a hundred thousand people there, they have tents where REO Speedwagon play, and Bon Jovi play and the Dead played there many times.

I think it's all about the experience. Camping in the wilderness is beautiful, but there is this experience you get if you're a music lover. You can go and see all these different bands and then sleep in a tent; it's a very memorable experience. When you're young with all your friends it's really special. The experience just keeps getting better with it going on for so long.

Ivan Neville: The festival scene? Well, ya know it's given us a place to play; it's given us an audience! Bands like Dumpstaphunk was like a side project at first. I had been away from New Orleans for a while doing this stuff, but when I was back in New Orleans to sub for my Uncle Art, who was one of the founders of the Meters—which was a funk band out of New Orleans, probably one of the most influential funk bands of the sixties—I was subbing for my Uncle Art playing with the Neville Brothers, which I had played with before as a kid, and I ended up coming back to New Orleans doing that and Dumpstaphunk; I started seeing what was going on in the scene. What got me in touch with all this was I heard my friend Theryl DeClouet, an old friend, who sang in a band with me awhile back. He was singing with Galactic at the time. He's known as the House Man. I actually gave him that name. So I started checking them out. Before that I was playing with Robben Ford. I missed out on a lot of shit because I was so wrapped up in getting high, so I was out of touch with a lot of stuff. So I was playing a gig with Robben Ford, and Soulive was opening up for Robben Ford, and this was one of their first tours, and I got to see them in their early stages. Then a few years later I hear about this band Soulive opening for Dave Matthews Band, and they started growing as a band, and I started checking out what they were doing, and I would sit in with them and the same with Galactic. So that got me exposed to this audience—and this is an extension of this whole jam band thing. The people that go and see these bands are the same people that go to these festivals. So out of that I was offered a gig at the Jazz Heritage Festival in '03, and I hadn't played the Jazz Fest myself in many years, so rather than doing just an Ivan Neville set comprised of songs I recorded from my history, I said I want to put together a band—who am I gonna get? I'll get my cousin Ian. And who for bass? I was thinking either Tony Hall or Nick Daniels . . . I'll just get both! So we ended up with two bass players, and I had a couple songs in mind, and we got a guy named Raymond Weber who rounded out the band, and we did our first gig in '03 at the New Orleans Heritage Festival. From that it was a side project we would do every now and again. We had this kind of super-funk group with what I thought was an all-star band. The name Dumpstaphunk came from a song I wrote with my two younger brothers called "Dumpstaphunk," and this band was funky as shit, so that is what we called it. So out of the Jazz Fest gig we played a few seasonal gigs around New Orleans, and then we did Bonnaroo in '06 or '07, and that was, like, our showcase performance that started getting us our fan base on this scene.

Jon Guttwillig [interview from the *Dartmouth Independent*]:
Look at Camp Bisco—it's the biggest electronic festival, outside of
Coachella, in the country. We could do twenty-five thousand people this year. Coachella does like forty thousand, so here we have
two electronic festivals doing somewhere in the neighborhood of
sixty-five thousand people between the two of them. That's Bonnaroo size! By the way, Bonnaroo is a jam band festival—we're playing it this year, and we've played it five times already. It's like all
these things that my band and a couple of friendly cohort bands
are putting their energy into are succeeding.

And the reason they're succeeding is that everybody is invited.
Everybody is allowed to come. You can come and do whatever you
want! We had Nasty Nas on our stage at Camp Bisco. And Snoop
Dogg! We feel like hip-hop is what made things more real. Before
hip-hop it was like, okay, walk out on stage, sing the hook, flash your
abs. Look at Incubus! Incubus is fucking huge! One of their songs
is a complete rip-off of Pink Floyd, and if their lead singer wasn't
as good looking as he is, they would be nowhere! They're the last of
this generation of what-the-fuck music that record companies were
able to force down the throats of the world. And now that it's over,
people actually want real music. They're actually paying for real music. And for a guy like me, who does not have washboard abs but
writes a pretty decent song every once in a while, maybe a good guitar solo every once in a while, it's like, hey, this thing can work out.

Greg Loiacono: That's what we love: the open-mindedness and
knowledge. Everyone that comes to these music festivals knows
so much about all kinds of different music: rock 'n' roll, bluegrass,
jazz, world music.

Reid Genaur: There are pluses and minuses to playing at festivals. The plus is that it's a blast; it's like a big party and it's great

exposure, since you typically play in front of larger audiences than normal. So it's a rush. You're on a huge stage with a huge sound system. The minuses are that you're rushed on and off stage. A lot of times the sound quality onstage is touch and go. You can't get your chi together, your head space together. The other challenge is it's like speed dating in some ways versus playing a whole night that is your show, where you're calmer and you have more room to explore range of repertoire and emotional texture. At a festival you feel obliged to do the one-two punch.

Larry Campbell: Well, he [Levon Helm] had lost his voice for a while and was getting it back and decided he did not want to go on the road and wanted to try to pull something off where people would come see him. He was playing with a blues band at the time. He tried it a couple times, and it worked out great. I had just left [Bob] Dylan at the time; he called me and asked if I would be interested in making music. So I went up and we did a couple of these things, and it was magic. The secret to the success of that [Midnight Rambles] is the complete openness and inclusiveness that permeates the place. The audience is part of the show—they are sitting around the band, the band is not performing; we are just in there with all these people. We're doing this, they're doing that, and . . . different people describe it in different ways, like a house party or going to church or any community gathering. I've been doing this for about eight years now, and I look forward to it every week just as much as I did the first time. It's only about having a good time playing music and no other nonsense.

Ken Hayes: I started a company in 1991 called Terrapin Tapes. What it was is a blank tape distributer for MXL and Sony and Panasonic, and we supplied the live tape trading community with their blank audio tape at more reduced prices than you could buy at the retail outlets. Then we went into live pro-audio gear: microphones, data machines, and all the needs of the tapers and the bands that recorded their shows live. That was awesome! It financed my ability to go on tour with the Grateful Dead. I would be on tour while some friends were back at my house, answering phone calls and packaging. It was a great experience—and then Jerry died! That changed everything. It was devastating. So myself, Bob Kennedy, and the folks from *Dupree's Diamond News*, a small Grateful Dead magazine, got together and put on Dead Head Heaven—A Gathering of the Tribe after Mayor Giuliani said no to a gathering in Central Park based on the cost and so on. So Bob, I, and *Dupree's* got together, and I had my database on three-by-five index cards of a couple thousand tapers and took out a small ad that said, "Dead Head Heaven—A Gathering of the Tribe." It was on Memorial weekend 1996, and it was beautiful. We had thirty-five hundred people. Max Creek headlined along with moe. and Strangefolk and the Zen Tricksters, and the event went really well and we had to move venues 'cause we outgrew it. The following year we went to Croton Point Park, and that is when we called it Gathering of the Vibes. So it went from Dead Head Heaven—A Gathering of the Tribe in '96, and in '97 it was Gathering of the Vibes. Here we are, sixteen years later, with twenty thousand people out front!

Peter Shapiro: The first "Jammys" was in 2000, so Wetlands was still going. In 2000 the pop band was very big—'N Sync, Backstreet Boys—huge, and we felt it was time to create an event that celebrated improvisational music and countered this teen-pop thing that was just dominating global culture. The idea of the Jammys was just putting everyone together. The awards were just an excuse to get everyone into the room, and then the real idea was to get those people to jam together in unexpected ways—unique collaborations that you wouldn't think would work. Some of them, of course, did not work. But when they did work it was like a Dead show, because sometimes it didn't work, but when it did work it was so special 'cause they weren't doing the same set every night for thirty shows. They were taking chances . . .

Oh yeah, the bands were resistant to playing with other bands with minimal rehearsal. What I have learned doing the live music thing is that once one person buys into it, others will follow. Here at Brooklyn Bowl, no one wanted to play here at first. It's a bowling alley in Brooklyn. Everyone was like, "We will come by next year." So when we first opened I had to ask some favors of Bob Weir and Warren Haynes and the Disco Biscuits and moe., saying, "I could use your help now—not next year . . . now!" So they did, and everybody loved it and everyone wants to play here, and that's true of almost anything, and that's how the Jammys were: at first no one wanted to do it, and then after it happened a few times and you started to get a list and be able to say the Black Crowes, Buddy Guy, and Steve Winwood did it, then it was easy. Then I did seven Jammys, which shows the magic that happens when people get together who have not played before and haven't rehearsed, with minimal sound check, and they get together and might play eight minutes that suck but then play four minutes that are great—and then it's worthwhile; it overcomes the eight minutes that sucked.

Dean Budnick: The next iteration of my larger idea in terms of introducing our scene to a wider audience resulted in the Jammy Awards, which ran from 2000 to 2008. It all began with something of a joke, because moe. manager Jon Topper kept telling me that we needed a Jammys to be our version of the Grammys. The more I thought about it, the more I decided he was right, and with the blessing and support of Wetlands owner Peter Shapiro, who had recently acquired Jambands.com with his brother Andrew and some other folks to be part of a larger web portal they intended to launch as Kind.com.

While we intended to give awards to deserving acts, in order to emphasize the grassroots nature of it all, rather than have all the decisions vested in the hands of a committee, we decided to open up voting to the public, via our website.

I remember that first year at Irving Plaza, Phish won the Live Set of the Year award (for their epic millennium performance at Big Cypress), but we were such a small event and they were on tour anyhow, so they couldn't possibly accept in person. But we let them know they had won, and Mike Gordon faxed an acceptance speech over to the venue, which we read, and it felt like such a triumph. In many respects it all came full circle at the final Jammys in 2008, which by then had moved to the Theatre at Madison Square Garden. We gave Phish a Lifetime Achievement Award, and they showed up together to accept it at a time when they were still broken up and had not performed together for nearly four years.

The other defining element of the Jammys was we set out to embody the improvisational nature of the acts we honored by presenting performances from musicians who had never played together before (and in certain instances had never met until the moment they took the stage on the night of the show). Peter Shapiro took particular pride in crafting these pairings (he had, after all, brought Hanson out with Bob Weir, Rob Wasserman, and Jay Lane for the tenth-anniversary of Wetlands). I often had a hand as well. For instance, at that final show I put together an all-star jazz combo for Phish's Page McConnell that included drummer Roy Haynes, saxophonist James Carter, trumpeter Nicholas Payton, and bassist Christian McBride.

Another early favorite took place in 2001 at Roseland Ballroom, where we moved the show for years two and three. We opened with

Del McCoury Band, Robert Randolph, and DJ Logic performing "Swing Low, Sweet Chariot." Now Del hadn't soundchecked and had no idea what was coming, so watching his triple-take when Logic started scratching from a recorded version of "Swing Low" was quality entertainment all around (for Del included).

Roseland was a great spot for the Jammys because at some point they had built a second stage at a ninety-degree angle to the original stage, which was typically used for VIP seating. But for those two years we restored it to its original glory, as the locale for our house band (Derek Trucks Band, Tom Tom Club) and also the awards portion of the evening. Then in 2002 we closed out the night with a jam that spanned both stages and saw Bob Weir and RatDog joined by Trey Anastasio, Warren Haynes, Al Schnier, John Popper, Matt Abts, Mike Gordon, Robert Randolph, Skerik, and many, many more.

As the Jammys developed, Peter did most of the booking while I focused on the awards, and I also served as the evening's emcee, donning a tuxedo, handing out trophies, and prepping our guest hosts. After Moon Boot Lover's Peter Prince in year one (I did the show run-through with him while we ordered sandwiches from a nearby market), we also had Jim Breuer, John Popper, Phil Lesh, Robert Randolph, Mickey Hart, Bill Kreutzmann, Warren Haynes, and Grace Potter.

So what happened with the Jammys? I'll just say this: going back to the very first year, the Grammys organization was aggressive about what they deemed to be their intellectual property, claiming that we were violating a trademark. Well, I will grant you that Jammy does rhyme with Grammy, but my Columbia law degree also tells me that the key to any trademark violation is whether the public would be confused by an alleged infringement. And I am here to tell you that no one out there confused the Jammys with the Grammys. Still, by that time then-*Relix* publisher Steve

Bernstein, who had come to own Jambands.com and our stake in the show, became nervous about attorney's fees and agreed to a settlement. I'd be stoked to see the show return one day in some form . . .

Alan Evans: A festival like this [Gathering of the Vibes], I have noticed a lot of tributes to the Grateful Dead, which is great, and then there are all these other elements being put into it, and that is what is great about this audience. Like, for instance, we do this thing at the Brooklyn Bowl every year—we do two weeks where we see everything from straight-up hip-hop artists and in the same night you see Derek Trucks or Warren Haynes. There are as many people cheering for Questlove as there are for John Scofield or Talib Kweli.

It's so diverse. I have looked back at the people Peter Shapiro pulled in from day one, like Amy Winehouse, he has had some of the biggest, most incredible pop acts to the greatest fringe stuff that is out there . . . and the underground Brooklyn salsa bands . . . just a huge range of music.

I think why people come to the festivals is it's nice finding bands and artists you've never heard of that are really good and to catch up with people you don't get to see often. For instance, we were at High Sierra a few weekends ago and we saw this band called Red Beret and they were killin' it—and come to find out they live down the street from me! I like to do the Bear Creek Music Fest—that is where we see a lot of our friends. And the Jazz Fest every year—we have known these people for thirteen years, so it's like a reunion.

Steve Kimock: If it wasn't for the festival scene I wouldn't ever see a band! I'm either working (like I will get to see the opening act tonight for a minute) or I'm home with the kids, so at the festival you get to see all the bands and everybody. I'm also okay with the idea that the festival scene is 99 percent social; it's not so much about the music. But the music is important to me. It's what I do.

Bill Kreutzmann: I love it! I love the amount of music that's getting played, the amount of bands that get to be seen and heard. It's a wonderful place for people to get together. I think the three-day festivals are great—people can stay there, they don't have to drive, they camp, and there are all kinds of interrelations that are really cool. It's basically a community we don't get to have outside of festivals. I really like it a lot.

Tim Carbone: I think it's essential. I don't think the bands could survive without the festivals. You get paid a little bit better, and they become, like, anchor dates. You need those anchor dates so that you can count on a certain amount of money and a certain amount of exposure. Then you fill in the blanks. As far as the scene amongst musicians, to me it is one of the greatest things, going to these festivals. We will run into other bands that we have played with, and we will be like, "Oh hey, how you doing, man?" There is cross-pollination. They call me the sit-in whore. For the most part I will wind up sitting in with almost everybody. Not so much recently. That cross-pollination is one of the things that I really enjoy about the scene and playing festivals. John [Skehan] is a sit-in whore too. And so is Andy [Altman]. The three of us.

John Skehan: I think, too, with the music of this band Railroad Earth and the quasi-acoustic nature of it and the organic vibe of Todd's songwriting, the music lends itself very well to an outdoor setting. I can remember early on rehearsing in the barn, and we were somewhat outdoors while working on songs like "Seven Story

Mountain," and thinking, "This is going to sound brilliant coming from a festival stage in a beautiful setting." There is something to the music that works well in that environment.

Andy Goessling: There are a lot of bands that we are friends with and hang out with. That's the whole reason why I like the festivals. I will wander to the farthest stage that I can find to hear a band that I've never heard before. Like to go hear Of Montreal or something like that. I'm never going to be able to see them otherwise. I don't necessarily know the band, but they had a big influence on me in the fact that I got to see somebody else's genre that I never would have had a chance to see. I mean it influences me and it's good for the other bands. They are not, like, friends of ours, but I definitely appreciate getting to see them. I just try to go see something that I've never seen before. I'll always go to, like, the third stage, and I will just try to make sure I see some people that I've never heard of. You never know. So I am just saying that there are two things: there are some people that you are friends with and that you sit in with, and then there are people that are working just as hard as you and are out there trying to get their message out and you go see them. And you are amazed and are like, "Wow, there is this whole other thing that I didn't know about."

Tara Nevins: Yeah, we're part of the festival circuit and we toured just a while ago with Railroad Earth. That was fun. There are all kinds of different things. And you know, it sounds really corny, but I find that it's happening more and more. And it might be because these festivals have broadened their scope. But it used to be very definitive. Bluegrass players definitely didn't dig old-time music. And old-time musicians definitely were not into bluegrass. There was a real division there. To bluegrassers, old-time music was so funky and "Can you even play your instrument?" And to old-timers, bluegrass was like, "Oh, you just want to play as many notes as you can play in one measure?" And there was this attitude, honestly. And I've seen it break down completely to where there is a real admiration from both sides. I've seen that with a lot of different kinds of music. At these festivals you're all just musicians, and it is truly the universal language.

It's really true. It's a microcosm. I feel all of these attitudes breaking down, and I see people really understanding what's cool and deep and soulful about all of these different types of music. Because let's face it: all of the musicians that are playing are playing something that has really touched them. Anyway, thinking about it like that, the whole festival thing broadening all these different musicians in one place at one time putting out this music has probably really contributed to that breakdown of attitude—certainly between bluegrass and old-time. I think it's a really healthy thing because old-time music is the foundation of bluegrass, and then all the music that came from bluegrass, all the jam-grass, it all stems back to the same thing. And then there's the Cajun and the Zydeco. Then we're playing some of that. It's just all one big really cool melting pot. I think there is a real appreciation that has developed.

Jason Ott: The energy is really the best part. When all the people are together and you get that community environment, that's really big in the jam scene, and what we've noticed from the jam scene in festivals from the people is incredible. We strive to match their energy when we play; it's almost a game of back and forth, so it's a huge amount of energy coming from awesome people.

Tara Nevins: In some cultures the music and that whole thing is just an everyday part of life. In a lot of places it's just not. People just work; their nose is to the grindstone. And you know, I think when people go to these festivals, for a lot of people, it's like a rebirth almost. It's like a regeneration of some kind of spirit. And definitely the festival thing really captures that and fosters that. So we were always really drawn to festivals.

David Gans: It's still there in music festivals, I think. I've had the good fortune for many years to play many festivals year after year. I've played the Magnolia Spring Festival and watched multigenerational families come into that thing and kids that would come up from toddlerhood and into this music and become fans of this music and become players of this music. They would see this kind of engagement. They would be out there when Donna the Buffalo is playing their set. They would hear all different kinds of music, and they would pick the music that they like and stick with it and engage with it year after year. The same deal with the Gathering of the Vibes up in Connecticut—it's a multigenerational, more Dead-oriented thing, and it's great to see grandparents and their kids and their grandkids there year after year. So the experiences are available; the whole world is just a different place. The sixties was just this magical window, and I was fortunate to be near it but not really in it. I was a little too young to be part of the San Francisco thing; I was an immature kid living too far away, didn't have a car, ya know. But I went up there and hung out in the Haight a few times, got to go to the Fillmore once or twice and stuff, but I was more attached to the media version of it. And there were a lot of media pandering to that vision and promoting that vision at the time. Nowadays music isn't the center of the culture like it was. When I was a kid and the new Bob Dylan record came out, everybody you knew . . . somebody in your scene would get that record, and you'd all get together; you'd just fucking all listen to it. We don't even consume music the same way anymore. People listen in their private pods, they listen on the subway, they listen in the car, they listen while they're playing games, they listen—you know, it's like music is not the shared cultural focus now that it was then. In those days everybody you knew, it wasn't everybody, we were this incredibly tiny little minority, and we were loud and enough of a market . . . the whole goddamn culture started focusing on selling us our own shit back to us, you know. We did change the world in that sense . . . the Beatles became huge pop stars and then took advantage of the power that gave them to mature and expand and start writing about adult themes and promote the idea of loving and being kind to each other. And *their* psychedelic experience and *their* attempts at enlightenment they shared with all of us and inspired the rest of us to try and do things like that too. The whole culture has gone back to materialism; the pendulum of selfishness has swung back the other way, the drugs that we take are different drugs now. It's a very different world, and it's a lot harder to find it, but I think that people are finding their truthful experiences—they just may not be musical.

Sharing the Groove

Trey Anastasio [from *The Phish Book*]: For years I've harped on the notion that a group is greater than the sum of its parts, and almost all the music I like demonstrates that. I don't usually like big solos, but I love King Sunny Ade, Bob Marley's band, the Dead, King Crimson, and James Brown's band. They're the greatest bands ever because they use tiny little bits of harmony and rhythm and make a web or mesh out of them. Those bands are bigger than ours, though, so weaving those webs is harder for us, and we've been experimenting with how to do it since 1994 or '95, when we were doing a lot of "Including Your Own Hey" exercises to make us all equally important to the improvisations. The big frustration of 1996 was that we were still basing everything around "big guitar solos with backup band," or "bass player trying to keep up with frantic drummer," or "keyboard player in background until emerging for big solo." The goal is to have each of us playing with an ear on the other three while feeling completely fulfilled . . .

When we're communicating, the audience hears what we're thinking as though they were inside our heads. But if I can't understand what somebody else in the band is doing, then nobody in the audience can either. The only reason we're here is because we've all experienced moments when we've transcended our egos and the music has taken on a life of its own. That's what brings people together for a Phish show.

Béla Fleck: Well, I remember Phish used to invite me out to play with them pretty often, and they were always trying stuff. One day they went and did an opera on stage and the next day come out and do bluegrass on one mic in front of ten thousand people or more—they were so brave. When they would ask me to play they would say, "We came up with these weird chord changes and we think you can play 'em." They were so creative. They would create these musical exercises to do during shows. One of them was where one person would start a pattern, and once he had locked down the pattern it would move to the next person and they would find a pattern to play with it that interlocked but was not the same, until all four players/patterns were working together doing this! It created these circular jams that I thought were genius. A simple idea, but after fifteen minutes this thing would have morphed into a brand new thing.

I just know that when we get into stuff, we like to trade phrases a lot. So one person will play, then someone plays off of what that person just played, and we go around and around to see where we get with that. I think the blood coursing through the band is the rhythmic connections, so that when we lock in and are locked together we're feeling each other through the rhythm at all times, and that's the primary bond. Our music has a lot of soloing in it. What I like about Phish is they found ways to improvise without soloing, because soloing gets boring. It's always fun to try and play your best and try something you never did, but a whole night of music—how much do you want to hear yourself doing that?

It's arguable that it's healthier for musicians to have a lot of different people to play with as opposed to, like, in relationships when its arguable that it's not gonna be good for your relationship if you stray out of your relationship. But it takes a lot of maturity in a band to step back and let everybody do their own thing, 'cause you never know if they're gonna come back when they do that. I've definitely been threatened a few times by my own fears about Victor [Wooten] in particular because he is such a beloved player and does everything really well. So I think, "I don't know if he'll come back," but he always does. That's the great thing—we do have that long relationship, so when he does come back I know he values what the Flecktones are.

Marco Benevento: It was the hook-up between Mike [Gordon], Joe [Russo], and myself before Trey [Anastasio] came along. Even before the three of us got hooked up, Mike was also on the label Ropeadope when he had some solo projects going around 2003, and he was looking for a drummer to do some things with, and the guy from the label recommended Joe. Then Joe had a session with Mike and their relationship started. Somehow it became a trio, where Mike wanted to tour and just decided to use Joe and I. Then we did some shows together and did some Phish songs and played some Mike songs and did that occasionally for about a year or two. Then, as far as Trey, I was sitting in my apartment hanging out with my friends, and my phone rings and it was Trey, and he said he was in Brooklyn working in his studio and I should come down and meet him 'cause we were gonna do some shows. It basically happened liked that. Then we found out we were gonna do a show together in front of a thousand or more people a night for three weeks. It was great—I loved it!

Bob Weir [interview from *Relix: The Book*]: I tend to write the kind of music that I want to hear, so it's my kind of music. If I can be evangelical about it here for a moment, it's gratifying to see people doing that. That's our legacy, and I'm thrilled. Not that they need our go-ahead. . . . As far as I can see, it's all good. I mean, we didn't develop this approach to music for no reason at all or as a conscious ploy or marketing tool; we did it because it's fun and interesting and leaves the music wide open for development from night to night and also from moment to moment. It's gratifying to see other people doing that. The more people who play like that, I think, the better. It's not like this is new. The jazz people have been doing it for years, and it's an American tradition. We're just bringing it into popular music a little more than it has been seen for a while.

There used to be more room for improvisation in popular music in the thirties, for instance, when the dance bands were hot. That was the ultimate improvisation happening then. Those were jam bands—the Ellington Ensemble, Count Basie, Fletcher Henderson, all those people. They were jam bands. So what we're doing is not without precedent. Still, it's great to see it come around again 'cause that means I can listen to a lot of bands and really enjoy it. When somebody's playing something fresh, you can hear it. And there's nothing else that supplies that punch. No magnificently rendered road performance is gonna amount to something that's happening right there for the first time. I like to live my life like that, and I like to see other people live their lives like that. I think that's the way it should be.

Eric Krasno: If you listen to the Grateful Dead or Phish, there is a lot of that influence that comes through. When we started Lettuce I remember going to see Phish early on; my brother knew them and I had met them a few times. A lot of the jam sections they would do, it was really like they were playing elements of funk or this and that. When we started Lettuce it was more about funk, but the thing we took from them was you can take it out there and get psychedelic and stretch, and these people, this audience, loves that; they get into it and get excited that they are a part of something that's totally inspired by the moment. They are bringing in an energy and feeding off all the other energy. That's what really impressed me—that they were able to do these deep, well-orchestrated parts and then go into these long, improvised sections. I was a fan of that part more than anything. They were able to touch on something as a group that was very unique to them. No one sounds like those four people together, and that is what I dig about bands in general. I think that is what this scene promotes. People get together and create something that is not packaged for commercial sale. People are out here doing what they love to do, and that is just inspiring.

John Bell [**interview from *Swampland***]: We all started together. As far as real bands and working musicians, we were just kids when we started. That's a big part of it. You didn't come in wielding some big ego or this pretentious sack of experience you thought you had. Nobody was like, "Hey, I'm a songwriter. Don't fuck with my song. This is how you play it." It was always collaborative with us. It was cool. We didn't have anything to protect or lose. The original four of us was a social experiment that included playing music together for a way of expression or focus. It's still that way twenty-five years later. One key element is we share the songwriting equally. It sets the stage for not letting anyone feel too much responsibility or getting too big for their britches. It's real. It's on paper, and that's how royalty payments come through, but that's symbolic for us.

Jimmy Herring [**interview from *The Examiner***]: Sometimes it depends on how far away the audience is from you. That's like only one example, because sometimes the reverse is true. Sometimes they can be far away and you still feel the connection. But in general it helps if you can be closer to them. I like when they're real close. I mean, literally, in clubs they're gonna be right where that flower pot is. And sometimes they're so far away. But sometimes you can overcome that and you can still feel the connection. Their energy is important to what we do. You just have to go in there and see how it goes. You play until you find out what happens, you know? Either way you're gonna do your gig, you're gonna do your best. And we always try to do our best and play the best show we can play regardless of what the circumstances are.

The fans for this group are so wonderful. You can feel their support; you can feel they're there with you and they encourage musicians to try stuff that they've never tried before. Like when you get into an improvisation, if you go into something you've never tried before, they seem to be able to tell. And they seem to be with you on that. And they also like groove improvisation. And some people call that a jam band or whatever, but I don't really know what that means, 'cause categories are funny like that. But I do know that this crowd loves it when the group is one living thing. And that's what this group does. Some bands just play rhythm with a guy soloing on top, which can be cool too. Everything's got its time and place. But this group doesn't necessarily do that. Even though I might be the guy playing on top a fair amount of the time, what they're playing affects what I play. I don't ignore them when I just go, when I leave a space—if I play a phrase like a sentence, and then I leave a space—I listen during that spot, and it affects what I'm gonna play next. And vice versa.

Warren Haynes [interview with *Murf*]: Well, I think the type of music we play and the type of people we are and the type of people we attract, all those things are interrelated. And it's not pretentious music. It's very organic music, and people that come to our shows have that organic quality in common with the band. You know we're . . . we're just all about hanging out and having a good time and playing music and listening to music and into being a good vibe, you know. . . . It's hard, the larger scale you do that on, the harder it becomes, but it's really important to us that we maintain that kind of vibe 'cause of all the experiences we've had through the years. It's really weird when the band is entirely severed from the crowd . . . and it's a hard thing to gauge how much energy is coming from the crowd. The crowd is responsible for a large part of the energy on stage. You know we play entirely differently in front of an audience than we would play if we were just in an empty room.

Vinnie Amico [interview from *In Music We Trust*]: It's pretty much all about the vibe. If the vibe in the room is really good, usually it is a lot easier for us to play. We don't have as much work. It tends to be easier. You're getting that feed from the crowd because they're really into it. It usually makes our jobs funner and easier to play. All of a sudden everything is clicking because people out there are really into it, we're into it, and it's just a whole. It's just kind of a whole. The better the vibe in the room, the better we play, and the better all-around show it ends up being.

Rob Derhak: They [the audience] don't realize, for me at least, how much control they have over what my mood ends up being like.

Chuck Garvey [interview from *Swaves.com*]: I think it's kind of like we made this little club and we have all our own inside jokes, and just the kind of things you have with friends from high school or college, where there are just a couple of guys who have been through a lot together, and for better or worse you're broth-ers. Definitely there's a sense of humor thing which is a big part of it, and then another part of it is simply creating music and making art. It's hard to do with friends, it's hard to do with family, it's hard to be in business together, but I think the sense of humor and friendship is what makes the business aspect of it or the work of it easier. As long as you balance the two things, you're going to enjoy yourself. So I think it's always kind of like a balancing act like that. You can get away with jokes, but you also have to concentrate and support each other when you're actually working. We just kind of—over time and a lot of miles of traveling and whatever—we struck a balance in how we do that. And keeping it fun is definite-ly a big concern for us.

Ivan Neville: The thing that comes to mind with me is gumbo. When I was growing up gumbo was everything: chicken, seafood, sausage, seasonings—everything you got. I'm sure it came from someone having a small amount of a lot of stuff and you put it together and have one big meal. That's New Orleans. You have all these different cultures down there—you got French, Native American, Italian, African, and then the Creole people and the Cajun people; it's just one big gumbo. You got brass bands, which I think is funk, then the Dixieland, the other jazz, and then you got bands like us.

Dylan Savage: Psychedelic roots reggae comes from the music we listen to, then comes into our music. One thing that differen-tiates our band from a lot of other reggae bands that you might not see on the festival circuit or don't jam as much: we like to jam. It's a different kind of jam based in the reggae esthetic, which is more soundscape building and a big part of that analog equipment. That's a big part of our sound. If I were to describe what kind of music we play, it's like 1970s-inspired improvisation psychedelic reggae that revolves around a good song. That is a part of all of our influences coming together. The old gear makes it a certain style of music that if you listen to, like, the Grateful Dead, that was the first I knew about keyboards, and now we have that sound in our band. North American music I guess.

Stephen Perkins: I was telling the guys in the band, to me that's where Jane's Addiction should belong, is stretching stuff out. We took a ninety-minute set and turned it into two hours, or we took a sixty-minute set and turned it into ninety minutes by extending all the guitar solos, by extending all the drum intros, and the audience was open for it. Mickey [Hart] was there, Elvis Costello was there, and it was just a wonderful night. That was a great night for me because it really gave us a chance to stretch. We did Pink Floyd's "In the Flesh," we did a little bit of "Ripple," we did "Sparks" by the Who, and it gave us a chance to spread our wings a little. We love the power of a punch but the caress of a kiss.

Michael Travis: In 2004 String Cheese was kind of creatively fizzling. I had pulled out my horses; I was like, "I'll drum for your band," but everything was kind of a little rotten at the core. No one cared about it anymore somehow. I had been thinking and feeling this and not voicing it, and I didn't know what to do. But Billy [Nershi] voiced that we should get a percussionist. I had been doing a lot of that with the double-handed half drum kit, half-conga thing. But there's always a part where I thought, *God, if there was a tambourine or cowbell right now or a shaker it would just make everything soar somehow.* I felt like we were ending the era of our vigorous five-piece school of Phish improvisational style, and I was like, "Why not check this out, you know." It's gonna have a bigger, "bodier" feel, but I was down. I knew the guy too, 'cause he sat in with us in '96—Jason [Hann], at High Sierra—and he just had this way of addressing every style perfectly. So I thought, *well, if you're ever going to get a guy,* and Billy said we should get a percussionist, and I said "I'm down. I'm down if I can pick the guy," and I just looked him up on Google—remembered his name, and looked him up—found him playing in a Santana cover band. I said, "Do you have Jason's number?" and they said, "Sure." I called him. Of course he remembered me, hit it up; he would come out for practices for String Cheese and stay at my house. And when he'd stay after String Cheese practices we'd just jam in my room. I had done a lot of double-handed tapping on the seven-string bass, so I'd just be tapping along and he'd be playing drum kit, and we'd be jamming. Then I had a loop pedal, and we'd loop it, and he said if you want to check out really serious looping, the program Ableton Live is the only way to go. He took the time to just get an Abelton rig going with a simple pedal, and I started doing that. Then I started adding a keyboard with a normal guitar and normal bass. Then a couple months into it, maybe the second practice session with String Cheese—I had always wanted to have a duo, where I was playing tonal stuff—and I was like, "Oh my god, this is the duo."

Then we just took it seriously and knew we were working towards a duo, but we worked on it for like more than a year before we played out our first gig because we just really wanted to hone it. At the time computer technology was just not up to par with keeping up with our CPU demands, and then when the Macbook Pro first came out, all of a sudden it was like, "Oh, we can do this." We just kept adding things and honing things and rebuilding our template and adding tricks and tools, and then we felt ready at Sonic Bloom, which is a festival my band, Zilla, throws every year. Then we played our first gig, and it just became obvious that it could have legs, and we really started pushing it. It was just so over-the-top dream-come-true for me to be able to play guitar in front of people.

On an airplane I'll describe it [EOTO] as live techno, but to a more honed audience I'd say it's live improvised dub-step house-glitchhop and trance, more honing into the individual styles we focus on. We've been in a dub-step phase lately. It's the new punk, in a lot of ways; it's pretty amazing stuff. It's the edge of the edge; it's barely music. It's this neo-tribal, overwhelming catharsis feeling.

It's the most gnarly, edgy music, but it's majestic dark, not angry dark. It's not the punk guys, like, "My parents wronged me, now I'm gonna tell you about it and you're gonna be angry too." It's this vast, vast . . . it encompasses everything in the dark that's ever happened on the planet, and in doing so you're also encompassing the light, because the dark comes below the light. For me it's just my random lexicon ramblings but very, very profound music in my world. And there's this certain group of sixteen- to nineteen-year-olds that are just eating it alive. Dub-step deejays are commonly doing eight hundred to two thousand tickets around the country. Bassnectar, who is doing predominately dub-step at this point, is doing six thousand tickets per night. It started in England, and it's a very specific formula: 140 beats per minute, with a half-time snare, so there's lots of double-time information, and then the bass tones have a big sign wave on the bottom, lots of stacks with a square wave, and maybe a synced saw wave above that. It's these big, huge, raking tones that sound like dinosaurs eating aliens. I had a moment the other night with this guy Excision, who is one of the great purveyors of dub-step, that I remembered all my past lives at once, in an instant, by this note that he hit. It's taking synthesizer tones to this whole other level, where there are sounds that are triggering DNA and emotional and spiritual information in your body that you can't even imagine or understand where it's coming from, but it's just these tones that are triggering stuff in people. It's so dark; it's this new teen angst music, and these kids are getting all this stuff out. Really exciting. I just feel like we're on the very, very cutting edge of something, and I can be a contributor, both of us can be a contributor to this new music that's never been heard before, by me just spending the time sculpting a new tone before a show and then dropping it on the audience. We're in a position where we don't have to spend days producing a track to give it to a deejay to play. We can do it that night.

It's all improv—I mean we do it all improv—but production-wise it's very, very meticulous. We have these highly deliberate pieces of music by these cats that can spend all the time in the world making it exactly impactful the way they exactly want to, and if they're not done, they'll just go to sleep, wake up the next day, and do it until it's perfect. So we're constantly reaching to this goal that is unachievable and trying to get as close as we can in the moment with no preproduction and no prethought or even pretalking about it. We don't talk about music on the road; we don't even listen to music. We just step up and go [makes explosion sound].

Mickey Hart: Everything is about feeling. You have to break down rhythm—whether it's machine driven or human driven—into a feeling. Does it create some kind of euphoric feeling? Does it make you feel good? The world is moving faster, it's stricter, it's more efficient in some ways; more clockwork is being achieved in the culture, so that is reflected in the music also—there you have your electronic music. Machines are getting smarter and humans are brighter on how to dance with these machines, so eventually that is another kind of music. Then there is the acoustic music, the archaic music. My world has one foot planted firmly in the archaic world of drumming and the making of the rhythm without any kind of ally, then the other deeply planted in the digital domain, and I dance between them at the same time. A lot of my friends now were born digital. They don't even remember an analog world. I find great pleasure in the archaic world of skins and sticking an object and getting this magnificent sharp sound, but now I'm able to combine that with the digital effects.

Rob Eaton: Music is all about emotion. The emotional content you put into it and what you get from the audience. I think people who go through the motions and are not using their soul to express what they're playing miss the boat. I think some of the greatest musicians of our time or even times before that are all able to put their emotions into something you can hear or feel. And not everyone can do that. Garcia, Neil Young was one—they weren't the best technical players, but you could feel what they played. There are some jazz players that play great, but none of it means anything. The great ones are the ones that connect the energy with the soul and the emotion to the listener. The Dead was filled with all that; that's what made it so special. That's what the jam bands are. Without the Dead they wouldn't be here. Phish and all those bands took the model the Grateful Dead used in almost every facet—how they jammed songs in and out of each other. That context was something that happened back in the day. So you look at Umphrey's McGee or Phish, and that is a blueprint of the Grateful Dead, and it's all over the festival scene.

Scott Murawski: One of the things about playing without a net and going into the free-form things and us being one of the earlier rock bands to do that is that you really detect this thing that happens where we are no longer in control of what is going on and the music is playing us and it's the entire energy of the entire room that is playing us and so that "everything" affects the music, including the audience. Very few musicians who improvise say they get it from the audience at that very time—and I think we do. If they are heavily dosed, then that will affect how we play. If they are all doing X, that will affect how we play. If they are all on coke, that will affect it. Without ever being conscious of it, when we go into the improv things, we are reacting to the energy—whatever it is, even the audience or our own stuff; whatever is going on at the time in the world. And for me that is some of my favorite stuff: when I'm the spectator watching.

Jeb Puryear: Strangely enough, even when you're playing old-time music and you're playing the same tune over and over again, you always feel like you're improvising. It's incredibly subtle because each little rhythmical nuance is like your form of expression in old-time music, and it's sort of the same with Donna the Buffalo. Like, some of our songs have a set pattern, but even within that very set pattern you tend to nudge the groove here and there. You know what I mean? Against or with it. For some reason I feel like the entire time it's got a sense of freedom to it. You're not nailed to this part even though you're playing the same part.

Tara Nevins: It's like you get in a trance and you ride it. You ride this wave, and then it ends. And you've all done this thing together, and that's how it's different. It predates bluegrass, and that's how it's different than bluegrass. So when we evolved into Donna the Buffalo, we took that whole trance-find-the-wave-and-ride-the-wave thing into Donna the Buffalo on our electric instruments. But now we have to step out and take breaks, which were really different for us—you know a very new thing and a very new way of communicating: letting the whole groove go behind you and all of a sudden stepping out and playing a break. It was really different and new, and I think that for many years what was really good about us was that we weren't the best at taking those breaks and that wasn't our real thing. But I think what really connected us with people was sort of the message in our songwriting. We just had this little trance thing and this groove thing, and it made people dance. People danced. Even at a crummy show, people just danced and they liked it even if our breaks weren't great or . . . you know what I mean? And it's just evolved over the years to where we can take breaks better and stuff like that.

When you're taking a break, though, when you're really taking a break, you're really stepping away from the crowd for a minute and, like, expressing yourself, and then what happens is everybody is listening to what you're doing and is tuned in on some level to what you're doing, and then they start traveling with you on that break. And if you rise, the whole band rises with you. And if you come down, the whole band comes down with you. If you come down, there may be space for you to come down. So there's a journey when you're taking a break. But when you set out to take your break you're definitely stepping out, and you're almost being brave by saying, "I'm leaving this thing now. I'm going here with it. I might fall or I might not or whatever." But everyone is supposed to go with you and take this journey with you, and that in itself becomes a groove. It becomes the whole thing and more in this journey, but it's very much still a wave and a groove. But you strike out kind of on your own, and that's a scary thing to get used to. I mean you strike out on your own and you're like, "Alright, see you guys. Here I go." And then, you know, you hope that everyone is going to like what you have to say. Everybody loves each other, and so you support each other and you go along with it.

And then sometimes you're like, "God, he's going on forever." Sometimes that happens too and you're like, "Okay, I'm sticking with you. I'm sticking with you but I am . . . " Sometimes you'll break for a long period of time. You'll be taking a break, and the way we do it in our band is, like, a lot of times, if I start taking a break, I'll sort of be the one mostly taking a break for a while. But then Jeb and David on keyboards will join, and then we'll all be taking a break together at the same time. Then after a while, though, he'll still have something to say, and he'll always be going on longer than me, and I'll be like, "Alright, I have nothing left to say. I've said it. I've said all that I needed to say." So then you have to find your way back and say, "I am going to sit in this groove and support this journey, but I have nothing left to say anymore."

Larry Campbell: When playing with Bob Dylan, he has always been at his best when it's him and a guitar—you can't beat that. So if you're going to be the band backing him up, you gotta take the place of that rhythm guitar. This means your accompanying the Bob Dylan thing. It's ultimately about the focus on him; that's what it's supposed to be. That is how he is best presented. With Levon [Helm] it's a completely magnanimous situation, where all he wants is to have a good time playing music and wants everyone playing with him to have a good time playing music, and everyone is in it together. The more we share everything, the happier he is, and he exudes that. Most gigs we play, even tonight, we are always having people come in and join us. It's the joy of sharing that musical expression that drives this thing.

Tim Carbone: We've always felt that way, that everything serves the song, especially when you have a songwriter that is as strong as Todd Sheaffer. You want to make sure that the integrity of the song remains intact. A lot of times I feel that, when we go into the improvisations, each one of us is doing the improvisations. It includes all of us, always trying to stretch it just a little bit, making it a little bit different. Each night each song seems to be kind of like a fingerprint almost. That is one of the things that I really love about playing in this band: you have the freedom to do that, but at the same time you are still playing bona fide songs. These are really good songs. We always have that in mind.

John Skehan: You try to take a look. We'll always look for a space where there will be a point of expansion, whether it's one or two songs where things will just sort of stretch out and breathe a bit. Because we have Andy [Altman] here, who plays so many different instruments, we'll begin to structure the beginning of the set or a portion of it based on where his instrument changes fall. We move quickly from one song to the next if we want to keep a pace going in the beginning to come out with some impact and then realize, here is a spot for a breath you can have, here between this song, and that is going to work toward something that begins to expand and develop, and you come back out of that then with maybe another tightly knit arrangement or up-tempo piece.

Andrew Altman: That's something that puts a stamp on each show. Recently we've taken time to know that when there is a transition coming and we want to go from one song to another and maybe I need to switch basses or Andy needs to switch or whatever, we'll invent a segue before the show that we don't rehearse. Yeah. We kind of call an audible, if you will. We say, "We're going to do this," and when it's time to execute that in the set, that's always a little unknown as far as how it's going to come off. I like that flavor that it lends to the show, that element of uncertainty in certain places where we're trying to cover a change or something. . . . And sometimes you mess it up. I think that is also a reason why fans of this band and of others like it—I think they like that. They will forgive you if you mess up because they want to see that you are trying something different and that human element. It's not some polished thing. Not to say that we don't strive for perfection; we're top-notch executionists. I think people appreciate the fact that you're trying to do something different every time. They forgive you when you mess up.

Bill Kreutzmann: You can't not play music for too long—you start to feel funny. It's your art, and when you're not touching your art you kind of feel sick. Ask any musician—they will tell you about that.

Steve Kimock: My musical studies, which are not like usual studies—everyone has a different take on it; my own are more about harmony in its traditional sense and the history of it and the manifestations of species around the planet. What I learn about it, like, just trying to put two notes together so they will be in tune just to find the things as they are together. You look for it and you find it in the sound; it's a very little very specific thing. . . . What I'm looking at with the harmony, with the specifics of it, is things as they are together. The more you appreciate that, the more the things are everything until you look at the stage and the people and the sky and the lake and feelings, odd securities, and the whole thing is the things as they are together, and then you go in there with whatever little vibration you have and try to make that little tiny adjustment you can so the harmony of the whole thing is together. My studying music has allowed me very slowly and humbly over a long period of time to appreciate the things as they are together in that big gathering sense.

Perry Farrell: The sound has changed, the outlook on music for young people has changed; they don't see it as . . . for example, my children said to me: "I hate music" because I was pushing them too hard. But they didn't see the beauty in what I do, because some of the stuff out there is god awful, so I understand why they don't think music is that great. Just this year, about a week or so ago, I went and performed at their elementary school. We did about seven or eight songs. The first three songs, the little girls were scared and the boys just had no idea. Then halfway through they started fist pumping. Then they started grooving, and by the last song every kid got up on stage—they wanted to rock out with us. The entire stage was full of little kids, and even my own kids were up in front. They were proud and they got it. It was like a huge breakthrough for me. My kids really understood why I love music so much and how important music really is.

Reid Genaur: There is the core, the concept, the bones of a song that get set up in the middle of the room, and people start to circle around it and start to flesh it out in a literal sense. In some songs maybe someone has nothing profound to contribute, and others they have something so much more articulate to contribute. A lot of the way a song comes together is modality. A rhythmic change can make or break a song. The guys that I have played with for the past fifteen to twenty years have all contributed in ways that are sometimes over it, sometimes sublime, but it is cool to see that collaborative process. Then, in terms of the improv, I think we are good at it, frankly better than most, but we are also realistic about what we're trying to accomplish. So we don't spend hours a week and tens of hours a month rehearsing improvisation. We spend that time writing songs, performing those songs, and recording those songs. We try to keep it in perspective. I think we've been harder on ourselves to try and say something meaningful and not just play for the sake of playing, which, frankly, I think takes self-restraint. I remember hearing, I think it was in a Grateful Dead interview, "It's what you don't play" and not only what you don't play note-wise during an improv, it's what you don't play in terms of the length of the improv. The only exception to that in all fairness is some of the greatest moments come after trudging your way through boredom, and then inspiration hits. You have to just find that balance, I guess.

Mickey Hart: Using drums as a diagnostic or a healing agent is the most exciting frontier in music, and what vibrations put back into the system that is broken—like in dementia or Alzheimer's or Parkinson's. It reconnects the neural pathways and allows for people to come out of the darkness—at least while the vibrations occurred. We know now there is more to music than dancing. There is perhaps medicinal elements in the vibratory stimuli of music. The frontier now is science. What is the neurology of music? What does the brain look like before, during, and after an auditory jiving experience like music? And how to codify that and be able to know what rate and what frequency does what to, say, a diseased organ, for example, part of an Alzheimer's brain. The neural science of drumming is a miniature of what's happening in the universe. That's where we got the music from.

The only way I can share in that is through sound. Now science is honing in on the vibratory universe and how to connect humans to the vibratory origins—the vibrations of the body, culture, and the rhythms of nature . . . the whole universe. It's all like clockwork; it's very complex but moving very efficiently—and that is what nature does: move efficiently. That is why I love music so much. It makes me feel good and it entrances me; it puts me in sync—me and everybody else—and we all have a good time. Now science is keying in on some of the things we did in the Grateful Dead: when you jam, when you play music with someone else, you are taking a multidimensional complex issue and trying to beat as one, to be in sync, to be larger than the parts. Everybody brings to the stage their own rhythm world, who they are. There are different levels of jamming. There is puppy jamming, then there is deep-root jamming, where the group has really achieved group depth, something that is "in the now." That is the ultimate goal for anybody who is a skilled performer—to be able to play together in the now! And playing without a road map and not thinking, just staying there as long as possible.

Content Is King:
Recording the Legacy

Horace Moore [interview from *Bands That Jam*]: It was kind of interesting, because I grew up in southeast Georgia. All I had growing up was the radio and eight-tracks and just one record store. It was kind of Top-Forty oriented. I can remember back in grade school, high school, just getting worn out on the same version of a song. So when I got introduced to the Grateful Dead, once I got to college that was one thing that I really picked up on immediately—this is cool. You got this band who just goes into a show not really knowing where they're headed in a specific kind of way. They just let it happen every night. As a result you get these different performances that just have these moments of magic and typically don't end up on a studio kind of release. That appealed to me right off the bat. Then I started quickly realizing that if you wanted to listen to the show and relive it, pretty much immediately as you're going to the next show, you had to tape that show yourself or be hanging with some buddies who were doing that.

Rob Eaton: My first tape that I remember collecting was the famous [Grateful Dead] Fillmore '71 tapes, some of the best bootlegs around in '74. That's what everybody had. I taped my first show with a rigged-up tape deck I borrowed from my high school. I rewired it so I could put a real microphone on it. Of course it didn't work out too well, but I kept working on it and evolving with it, and by '77 I made some good tapes, and by '78, '79 they were pretty good!

Horace Moore [interview from *Bands That Jam*]: I kind of got introduced to the Dead by a dude named Tom Merrill who lived out in Colorado. He gravitated toward the taper thing immediately. We'd grown up together as well. He introduced me to that whole thing, and it just took off. That really segued into how I met Dave Schools. His first day of school at Georgia in the fall of '83, a friend of mine who was living in the dorm across the hall from him. He realized Dave had a lot of Grateful Dead tapes, called me up, and said, "Dude, you have to come over and meet this guy." So that was it. The whole magnetism of the taping experience really pulled me into that whole thing. It really opened up a lot of friendships, experiences, and opportunities for me down the road. It was destined, I guess, in a certain way.

Rob Eaton: Well, we had a lot of creative ways to get in. We've had girls with harnesses between their legs. The best, most creative but not too politically correct was the wheelchair, where you would have a guy in the chair with a blanket over his lap and hid the tape deck and mic stand in pieces to fit on the side. We would go early and through the handicap area, and the "cripple" guy wouldn't get patted down! Barry Glassberg was a genius. He would come in a three-piece suit and a briefcase with a tape deck, stand, and mic inside the briefcase. You had to be creative.

I remember at Dartmouth College, no matter how hard I tried, I couldn't get in. Back then it was the venue. The band didn't care, but they didn't go to the venue and say, "Let the tapers in." They would be saying, "No audio. No video."

There weren't many of us back then, maybe four to six people with a mic, at most. It was hard to get in too. You had to smuggle them in. There was Barry Glassberg, Jerry Moore—he was one of the first tapers and the founder of *Relix*. It was a very small community. We all knew each other and we traded with each other. It exploded in probably the early eighties, when people started buying tape decks. In '85 I made my last audience tape. I was getting tapes from the band through the sound board, so the hassle factor wasn't worth it. I still have a substantial collection. Dick Latvala and I were good friends, and I got a lot from him. The taping scene was a strange little world, and as it got bigger you'd have people show up with a tape deck, holding your cables, wanting to patch out, and you've brought mics and stands and have had to schlep it all in, and some guy wants to patch and call himself a taper.

Jeff Mattson: The thing from a nontapers' point of view was you didn't want to be sitting next to a taper 'cause they were really anal. You couldn't make any noise. At least if you're in a taper section, you know what to expect. But if he is sitting next to you in a regular section, you can't make noise or walk in front of him. It can be a real drag.

Rob Eaton: By the early eighties it got very . . . there were tons of tapers, and they would be up front, and they would have their mic stand, and that started to piss [Dan] Healey off 'cause he was looking at the stage in a sea of microphone stands. I think it was the fall of '84 when they had their first taper section to try to alleviate that, and they said if you're up front, we will throw you out.

That's when people used to get binaural heads with the mic built in. They put a bandana on it and put it up on a stand, so it just looked like a six-foot-three guy in the tenth row.

There are some really aggressive tapers that were really mean, and that gave all tapers a bad name. That's kind of what put us off the scene. They would go and find the perfect spot on the floor, even if it wasn't their seat, and when people came they wouldn't give up the seat. They would say, "Here, take these tickets and go sit somewhere else." They would do some very passive aggressive things to get that spot, and it put a sour taste in my mouth.

Jeff Mattson: Well, if you're a band, which is not the case in the jam band community, where you're doing the same show every night, there is not much point in taping show after show because they all sound the same, plus they probably want to put it out as a live album at the end of the year.

Rob Eaton: It's improvisational music, which is what the whole jam scene is based on—the jazz concept, which is no show or song is played the same, and there is no right or wrong way of doing it. So you can collect all those tapes and they are all valid to their own degree. Their own personality. So that's why you taped, because you didn't want to miss the "good one." That's why you taped a lot of them, although the tape never did it justice.

Horace Moore [interview from *Bands That Jam*]: The taping thing in the Panic world, one of the things I've heard the guys say and seen a few times in print as well: they get out to these shows in the Midwest and on the West Coast and they'd realize that people were already ready for them and knew the tunes a little bit because of the tapes. Friends connected with colleagues, groups of people that come together there. There would be people here that would see Panic, get some tapes, then go home wherever, out West, for the fall breaks, spring breaks, summer breaks. They'd take those tapes out there, and lo and behold, these guys get out there, and it helped them out already. A little premarketing way back when. It's definitely connected in with the whole community aspect of it. It's a fabric of friends sharing music.

Chuck Garvey: There was a big tape-trading community, where people would send shows cross-country just for the price of blanks and postage. A lot of the shows from Wetlands and other places got traded all over the country. So someone on the West Coast would hear these East Coast bands and know a lot about them.

Jim Loughlin: All those bands were like fillers on a Grateful Dead tape.

Al Schnier: Yeah, even Phish was, so back then it was like that. Somebody heard about a band as filler.

Jim Loughlin: The first time we went out and toured for, like, four weeks and wherever, we would show up, people would know our music.

Rob Eaton: It's free advertising!

Aron Magner [interview from *The Aquarian Weekly*]: The paradigm has shifted. There are definitely two very different schools of thought on it. Music is no longer a commodity. Everyone feels entitled to have free music at this point. It's so easily accessible—why shouldn't we just have it?

It's weird how whatever the Napsters of the world have done has changed that approach that buyers have to recorded music.

Maybe the price point was too high, and that's just what caused everyone to go with the free thing? Whatever it is, the times have unfortunately changed. You could either be stubborn about it or you could realize that in this present situation nobody really feels that they're going to buy music anywhere. You hope that they do still, but you also want the means to get the music out there, because that's the most important part. If you recoup your money, that's great, but if it means that only a tenth or a twentieth of the people are going to hear the music, then what's the point?

I'm not saying that we should give away all music from here on forward, but we're just trying to get the same deal that we talked about a few years ago. We're just trying to get the music out there and get heard. If you get a free CD, you're gonna listen to it.

Warren Haynes [interview from *Murf*]: I think it's a way of spreading the word to a different type of audience. You know, in the same way that the Grateful Dead did and all the bands that we mentioned earlier—coincidentally all allow taping and in fact encourage taping. We set up little taper sections. So you get there early; you set up your microphones, your DAT, and your cassette. I don't think it hurts record sales at all. I think in the way if someone's a fan of your band, they're gonna buy your records, but they also want stuff that's not available commercially. Then I think one of the spokesman for Phish recently said that as large as the whole scene has gotten now, that they credit it for reaching more people with their type of music than radio and MTV combined.

John Skehan: I think we have become so conscious and so hyperattentive to what is happening on stage—if it's a good sounding stage or a bad sounding stage—if it's difficult, you just do everything you can to think about playing. I think there have been moments too where we have come out of something and thought,

"God, that didn't work at all." And then our front-of-the-house engineer, Mike Partridge, will say, "That was the best show of the tour! Are you kidding?! That section you did or that jam was the best thing of all time!" And we walk away going, "I don't know."

Carey Harmon: You get over that after the first few shows. I've certainly forgotten about it. I see them [tapers] now and again and go, "Oh yeah!" But it's just such a part of this.

Andrew Altman: And they're taping all the other bands that are doing what we're doing too. So it's not like anyone is going, "I heard Railroad Earth mess up that one show," because you can find a million other shows of other bands doing the same thing. When you get taped it's all caught. And with other bands it has happened to them too. You erase it.

Andy Goessling: You think that you would be the best judge of your own show. But it has been proven over and over again that if you hate it or think it's your worst show and you listen to it later, you will be like, "What's this? Is this the show you hated from Montana? Oh, wow! This is really good!"

Jay Blakesberg: I was listening to a Terry Gross thing on NPR the other day, and she was interviewing some war photographers and about how, given their injuries, if they could, they would go back to Afghanistan and shoot more photographs. Basically what they were saying is that it was important to be a witness to changes in our culture. I do that on a different level. It's pop culture, it's music culture, but we're obsessed with music—at least I am—so it's important for me to be documenting. That's what brings me back. Not only am I documenting this pop-culture phenomenon called rock 'n' roll, but I like it. I think that if I was just going to see a band that plays the same thing over and over again, I don't know that I would maintain that intensity of wanting to document that moment. Some people stop and say, "Oh, I already have pictures of Jane's Addiction, moe., and Phish—I don't need any more." If only I knew then what I know now, I would have shot five thousand more rolls of film on the Grateful Dead than I did . . .

Okay, so how I got started: I was a teenage Deadhead in the 1970s. I had older siblings into the Dead, Zeppelin, New Riders, Allman Brothers . . . some of which is in your blood and some is a product of environment. I grew up in a town called Clark, New Jersey. The next town over, Cranford, New Jersey, the people were into AC/DC and Rush, and everyone in our town was into the Grateful Dead, New Riders, and Allman Brothers. When I was sixteen I borrowed my dad's camera and went to a Dead show— the Meadowlands Labor Day weekend 1978. I took some pictures and created my own memorabilia. I wanted to create photographs I could hang on my bedroom walls. I had no idea this is how I could make a living someday. I just wanted to take pictures. I had a dark room I set up in my closet, and eventually I started selling eight-by-tens in the parking lot at Dead shows for $1. I started taking my camera to concerts, then I became enamored and went on tour with the Grateful Dead. This is the eighties, and I took LSD, and it changed my life—my mind was blown. All of that comes into play: being on tour, being a Deadhead, and my interest in doing photography. Maybe it's somewhat of an alter ego. Maybe I'm Jimmy Olson in disguise. Then I started shooting Deadheads, and my friends and I were on tour. If I knew then what I know now, my documenting would have been different and grander—if I understood that documenting photography even existed. So I took a lot of pictures. I'm proud of what I did with the Grateful Dead. I moved to the Bay Area in the mideighties and I started submitting photos to *Rolling Stone* magazine in '86–'87. I had a friend that went to high school with the new photo editor of *Rolling Stone,* and I submitted for the Random Notes section, and they were like, "These are great, Jay, exactly what we need, exactly what we use, but we can't use you because we have never used you before." Catch 22. But then U2 did a free concert in downtown San Francisco during *Rattle and Hum.* Remember that movie? I'm in it. There's a great shot of Bono from behind the stage, and there's a guy through his legs with a Nikon and a mullet—that's me! The reason I knew this was happening was the Grateful Dead's sound system was the sound system for that. So Dan Healey was there; Don Peterson from Ultra Sound was there at this free concert in downtown San Francisco. So all us Deadheads knew this was gonna happen; there was a buzz about it going around. J. C. Juanis told me a week earlier about this happening. So I heard it on the radio and started packing my camera equipment and was ready to go when I got a call from *Rolling Stone* magazine saying they got my first assignment: "Go shoot the free U2 concert." That was my first assignment for *Rolling Stone,* and since then I've shot over three hundred assignments for the magazine that got printed— real assignments. That was the start of my professional photography career. Before that I shot for *Relix.* I did stuff with J. C. Juanis; he was a writer for *Relix* magazine. We—J. C. and I—did a column on San Francisco music—jam band music before it was "jam band music." So I was shooting, but scraping by. I lived in a house in Oakland with six other roommates. Starting to shoot for *Rolling Stone* changed my life. I worked really hard, met bands, managers, record companies, and got assigned things with the Grateful Dead, which is how I started shooting them professionally. Then post–Grateful Dead, J. C. introduced me to the Phil Lesh camp and I started doing everything with Phil. I did the most recent shoot with Further at Gathering of the Vibes . . .

One of the things that allows me to do what I do is the trust artists have in me. Bands give me access because they trust me to be in their dressing rooms. Many things that happen happen in rehearsal. When I was the tour photographer on the Dead tour in 2009 they had a rehearsal room, not so they could learn the music but to figure out ways to expand it. Phish does that, moe. does that, Umphrey's does that, Yonder—a lot of bands. Most people don't get to go in those rehearsal rooms, and I have been lucky enough to do that with a lot of bands. It's a really cool and magical place to be a fly on the wall. Most fans don't get to see that. I get to go in recording studios, dressing rooms, and rehearsal rooms. I get to take pictures of the bands in their homes sometimes. Now in the world of Facebook and social media everything is fair game, but you still need to know where to draw the line—what's okay to share and what's not. It's still the band's intellectual property. I get to shoot and be onstage because these bands trust me and I'm good at what I do, which I hope is part of it. I take good photographs, direct good video; I can work with these people and it's not a "groupie" thing. My favorite photo I ever did of Jerry Garcia is a really close face portrait of him. It was for a shoot for *Golden Road* magazine, Blair Jackson's fanzine. It was an article he was doing with Hunter and Garcia, and I went to the Dead office, and Dennis McNally, the band's publicist, put me in this tiny little office, and Garcia and Hunter sat in these two chairs, and I had to sit on the desk to shoot them because it was such a small room. When I shoot a band I shoot a lot with many different angles, lighting, color, black and white, but this time I only shot a half of a roll, and McNally walks in and says, "Okay, you're done." I shot half a roll of color and maybe two rolls of black and white in about three minutes. But people like Garcia, Neil Young, and Santana I've worked with over and over again, and when I work with them I want to be brilliant, otherwise I won't get hired again. So I want to get the most time and be the most creative, whether I have five minutes or five hours. But a band like that, they want it to be over; they have sat there for a while and just want it to be over. I'm working on cool lighting lenses or cool types of films; I want it to be a memorable image, an iconic image, for them and me. I think I've done that; I've succeeded, given the opportunity, to work with many artists . . .

If you look at my last book that came out, it's called *Traveling on High Frequency*. It's my thirty-year retrospect of 1978–2008. That book has twelve hundred photos in it. All my books have multiple photos in different spreads—it takes a lot to tell a story visually. If I go to a festival, there is not one photo that tells that story; there is multiple photos. I like to say I create and capture that magical musical moment. This year I have been to five festivals so far: Summer Camp, Mountain Jam, High Sierra, Harmony Festival, and now Gathering of the Vibes. I think these midsized festivals, they're not Bonnaroo, but to me these are really engaging festivals, and those bigger festivals might be right for some people, but not me. I carry too much gear, and I think there is too much music, too much distraction. I love moe.down: two stages right next to each other—you can see everything. I don't need 180 bands at a festival. Summer Camp has 60 to 80 bands; I only see 20. Like Lollapalooza, you have to walk through the city to get from one main stage to another. I like Gathering of the Vibes—all the music on one stage. I just went and saw Tea Leaf Green, and they blew everyone's minds—they are main stage material. I trust these festivals to bring unique acts to the stages. Orgone—amazing band. The Mother Hips played here on Thursday—amazing band. I think at a big festival, artists like that get lost. moe.down is great; it's so many great jam bands. You know what's really interesting is when the Grateful Dead were happening there were Deadheads who would only listen to the Dead or Allman Brothers, and there was so much less choice in the jam band arena than there is now. So people really vortex in the parking lots. All you would hear is the Grateful Dead or the Allman Brothers, literally, and now the jam band fans that come to these festivals are way more open minded than any fan from anywhere. At summer camp this year they had Wiz Kalifa, who's this hip-hop artist; he had ten thousand people watching, singing along to every word. These are tie-dye-wearing dreadlocked hippies, and they knew every word. They are music fans, engaged music fans, that don't just listen to jam music. They will go see bluegrass, hip-hop, electronica, Kings of Leon. There is all this music out there, and they are into it all— they are music fans. I think that you go to bigger festivals, and they want to go see the pop flavor of the month or the big name artist, and it's fabulous to go see Radiohead or Paul McCartney or Roger Waters or Prince at a festival like that, but I don't know if I want to brave seventy thousand people. I'd rather go have a more intimate experience with twenty to thirty thousand people. If I had to work it, I would, but I prefer smaller. High Sierra is an incredible festival—Summer Camp, moe.down, Mountain Jam. I love Mountain Jam—two stages right next to each other. Some of the most incredible music I've seen has been at Mountain Jam. Last year, Levon Helm's seventieth birthday party, he played three hours. He had Jackie Green, Warren Haynes, Ray LaMontagne, and Sam Bush—it was unbelievable. The other thing that these festivals create is opportunities for people to play together. For me, visually, photographically, film-wise, you are capturing a unique moment in time. I love when Warren Haynes sits in with other people. Grace Potter . . . Warren came out and played with Grace and it was . . . it tore the house down at Mountain Jam. That's why bands that jam have these opportunities to let people come in and sit with them and create those moments. It takes it even further than those individuals doing something new every night; it takes it to a whole new level to come in and sit with people. I think these festivals foster that environment and make that happen, which is a really good thing . . .

I don't think there was ever a definitive moment when I thought another thing was going on. I think the birth of these festivals had something to do with it. There is moe. and Umphrey's; there were other bands in the Grateful Dead family. I first heard moe. on a tour with the Other Ones and Hot Tuna, post–Grateful Dead '96, '97, '98—something like that. Phish, I got turned on to them in '93, but I was already a member of a cult called the Grateful Dead, and I couldn't join another cult called Phish. So I didn't really get dialed in to them until they hired me, and I became their photographer for years. But I don't do much work with them at the moment, although I'd like to. They're a band that really understands the value of documenting. The band, that is your legacy, and it's important not only from a historical pop-culture standpoint. The Grateful Dead make a significant form of revenue on their archive they started doing so many years ago. So if someone said to them back then, "We don't need to record your shows; they won't ever have any value or be worth anything," it would be a very different world. Same thing with today. I think these bands need to document everything. You never know what's coming around the corner. We knew nothing about YouTube ten years ago. Content is still king, so for bands to say, "No, we don't want to be filmed," for whatever stupid reason, it's just not smart. I'm not saying that because I'm Jay Blakesberg, hire me. I'm saying that 'cause it will benefit you not only for history—'cause if you're playing these festivals you have a place in pop-culture history. But economically, this could be your kids' financial future.

Official Taping Statement from Phish.com: What is the Phish and Band Member Taping Policy?

This policy was last updated in August of 2010, so please

read closely. This policy applies to Phish and the individual band members. Audience taping is permitted at all shows. Guest performances with other artists will be governed by that artist's policy. When performing at a festival or other event featuring multiple bands, that event's policy may override Phish's customary taping policy. When performing in Ottawa, all bets are off. That place is cuh-razy.

All taping is audio only with microphones only (no soundboard patches, no video) in the taping section. At most shows, a designated taper's ticket is required in order to bring recording gear into the show. The bearer of a taper's ticket is permitted to bring ONE audio recording device and ONE microphone stand/set of microphones into the venue. No video devices are ever allowed.

To record a show that is entirely general admission, a taper's ticket is not required. In an amphitheater with a reserved pavilion and general admission lawn, the taping section is usually located behind the mix position in the pavilion and a taper's ticket is required. In an arena or theater with a general admission floor and reserved stands or balcony, a general admission floor ticket is required. If there is reserved seating on the floor, a taper's ticket is required. Tapers' tickets are marked on their face with the text "taper." Tapers' tickets are usually sold only by Phish Ticketing (formerly Phish Tickets-by-Mail); they are not available from other outlets unless we specifically announce otherwise. Anyone found taping in violation of the above policy will be removed from the venue and unauthorized recordings will be confiscated.

Entry to the taping section at general admission shows is first-come first-serve; taping will be permitted on a space-available basis with any ticket. When the section is full, no additional equipment will be allowed into the venue. You have the best chance of getting a spot in the section at a general admission show if you are in line to enter when the doors open.

The enjoyment of the audience at a show takes precedence over recording efforts. This means that tapers should not require others to be quiet or otherwise interfere with their enjoyment of the show. If your neighbor coughs his way through "Tweezer," consider it extra percussion.

The Final Say:
A Few Words from the Fans

What Does the Term "Jam Band" Mean to You?

"A Jam Band is a group of musicians who not only allow the music to organically flow in the moment and be affected by the environment, stimulus, and the emotions of the musicians playing said music, but also the music is affected by the audience if played in a communal setting."
—*Jason M.*

"The term Jam Band to me means a type of band that is known for their live improvisations. Jam Band also means to me music that is about performance and about the love of music; it does not care about being commercial or popular."
—*Michael A.*

"A group of musicians open to shared improvisation, multigenre exploration, and unabashedly unafraid of taking the long road to get there, as the journey is reward itself. Often considers the

audience as an unofficial additional member contributing to the x-factor in live performances."
—*Eugene E.*

"The term 'jam band,' to me, means a band that is willing to take risks with their music during live performances instead of playing the same notes on sheet music that they recorded."
—*Daisy H.*

"The term 'Jam-band' to me means that you are submerging your-self into the creation of one's art, allowing your soul to dip itself into a meditation. As I often say to people, 'Dancing to Wide-spread Panic, is like making love to music.' There's something that allows me to Zen myself, and soothe when I'm down. I always go to shows sober, because I'm becoming intoxicated from what my ears and body are feeling and hearing."
—*Savanna C.*

"There's no more exciting 'live' music than a jam band. Hip-hop live sucks. EDM died in a warehouse in, like, 1992. Pop music has some flair, but there's no getting down. Jam band music, which to me also includes funk and jazz, is free-form and fantastic. You gotta get up to get down. How you gonna do it if you really don't want to dance?"
—*J. J. C.*

"Jam music, to me, is the essence of my life and friendships. Since I started listening to that kind of music, I have met so many new people, most of which are now very close friends. Being in a jam band is also the best way for me to express myself musically, be-cause every time I play a solo it will most likely be different."
—*Dylan B.*

"As I attempt to answer exactly what 'jam band' music is, I keep coming to the same conclusion: after playing and enjoying this music my entire life and performing in many bands, both jam bands and non–jam bands alike, it's a lot easier to say what a jam band isn't. There's a whole list of things a jam band, isn't that we could easily assemble, and a whole list of music and bands out there that just don't 'jam.' Many folks that do indeed play within the 'jam' genre don't wish to even refer to it as a 'jam band' . . . obviously the term has been overused or misses the mark for some people as a label for this music, but certainly whatever we choose to call it, it is agreed to have these elements we attempt to convey with the 'jam band' moniker. As I compare the lists of just what comprises this type of music, which bands are jam bands starts to feel pretty stark and obvious when you come across one in comparison to its non-jam counterparts. The ever-changing live LONG set-lists and breadth of live repertoire seems the most obvious off-the-cuff divergence with their non-jam counterparts. U2 plays the same set their entire tour. There's barely a fresh moment. (I've seen Bono grab his crotch at the same exact moment from night to night, and not even as a lyrical reference, in the same song played every show of a 150-show tour.) There are exceptions to rules, of course, as some bands (Dave Matthews Band perhaps) seem to straddle a line that does attract a jam audience, but most would say the music doesn't feel very 'jammy.' I saw Alanis Morissette the other night in Denver, as I do actually love her music. No matter how much she might use improvisational techniques or elements in the act of composing her music, this is obviously not jam music. It's note for note, every night striving for a perfect execution of a composed plan that'll get close and sometimes hit the goal. Adele last year wasn't a jam either, nor the Nine Inch Nails show. Barry Manilow and Neil Diamond do not play jam music, but they really are great composers. Roger Waters's The Wall this

past year was one of the best productions I've ever seen, but it's
not a jam concert, even at close to three hours of music. But what
about the Band? Or Led Zeppelin? Most would agree they're not
quite jam bands. Both phenomenal musical acts, both with stages full of great players and terrific music that helped prime the
pump of jam music's extended soloing and perhaps somewhat the
noodling, but far removed conceptually from the adventuresome
live performances and open-ended compositional styles that jam
bands bring to their live performances and overall vibe as a band.
What about Zappa? Nope. While many jam musicians love Zappa
for inspiration, he had an exact result he looked for in his perfec-
tionist style of composition, and that excludes him. Trey could
have been just like that with his compositional style and has been
regularly critically compared to Frank Zappa, but his band is a
jam band, and the compositions they write sit within a breathing,
evolving form that stretches itself each night to continue growing
as a collective chemical reaction between the four of them and
their audience, and makes for adequate space for altered forms of
the music they play, perhaps slower and faster approaches, fresh
moments, and moments we can only describe as supreme musical risk. Those elements were always part of the Grateful Dead's
music. Risk. Performance is always risky . . . but this is different.
This happens only in the NOW. This musical risk is inherent to
the form in a way that mirrors true presence for us as humans.
On the extreme edge of 'Nowness' is: open and sacred, vulner-
able and courageous, not without fear but courageously moving
forward through time with trust/faith that it will be okay. The per-
fectionism is intrinsic to the music's nature, not a composed setup
striving to an ideal. The music will be there, the jam will carry us
through it, and the other side will be larger than the sum of the
parts . . . sometimes."

—*Todd W.*

"A jam band to me is something that cannot be defined clearly. It is a freedom to explore music that has no boundaries and is not genre specific. A place where a group of musicians can explore new sounds and new arrangements with no restraints, relying on improvisation and the energy of the moment."
—*Ross B.*

"A jam band can be described as a group of musicians that sets out to create well-crafted music that is enjoyable and flowing."
—*Josh S.*

"I play in two bands, and one of them, Gray County, is a jam band. So I get to experience both kinds of approaches to playing live music: more structured than not, less structured than not. And while a good structured band has elements of jamming (specifically, there is room for change), a good jam band usually has elements of structure—in other words, a place from which you start your musical conversation. Which is what the term jam band means to me. The 'structure' allows a free-flowing exchange of musical ideas, what I perceive of as a conversation with music.

"I'm sure you've noticed that in everyday conversations between friendly folks, the topic of that conversation can move fluidly and easily from one to the next. You may start conversing about the weather and end up conversing about border collies. So, too, with a good jam band. The conversation starts in one place and ends up in another. And here is where structure frames a jam and makes it satisfying. Gray County performs 'Dr. Robert' by the Beatles. It starts out as a straight-up pop tune in F. But after the second chorus ('Well, well, well, you're feeling fine . . . ') we start a jam in F. Where it will go, nobody knows. (Except it will probably stay in the key of F. Pharoah Saunders would never imagine such a thing as a key signature, but most jam bands at least have a key center that their jams swirl around.) We usually start with a couple of solos—first from the violinist, next the guitarist is a usual format. But at some point (never the same place twice) the conversation begins. Guitar says, 'wha-wha-wha,' and violinist says, 'wha-wha-woo,' then the bass says, 'yo-wha-yo,' and so it begins. And frame comes back when everyone has said all they can think of on the subject of F, there is a subtle nod, and 'Dr. Robert' comes back from his cosmic trip. ('If you're down he'll pick you up, Dr. Robert.')

"The jam itself is mostly phrased in multiples of two bars. But even when adhering to that basic rock-and-roll idea, things get really interesting when you start having cross-conversations. One player picking up an idea from another even before the first player has finished his/her thought. Very much like the conversation you might have with someone you are very close to. Even as you are often delighted and surprised by what that person says, you also are familiar with their thought processes and can 'finish their sentences' for them. And when that is going on among four to five players at once, you get an amazing energy.

"A lot of 'jam' bands to me sound like a soloist being backed by a good rhythm section. Mostly you hear what the soloist has to say. And I love to hear good soloists and good, energetic backing. Yet that construct is like a congregation supporting a preacher whom they believe is getting to the heart of things (Amen, brother; yes, indeed; I believe that!, etc.). And while that kind of jam is fun, for me the really interesting jam bands are the ones who get to the point where everyone—the choir, the congregation, the accompanists, AND the preacher—are all listening closely to what each other have to say and are looking to support, extend, or expand upon the ideas that are swirling around the church. (Case in point: 'Dark Star' at Veneta, 1972. Wow. They just got out there!)"
—*Gary M.*

"A jam band is a band that is heavily influenced by improvisational styles of music and takes it way out there."
          —*Randi M.*

"The term jam band to me means a band whose performance is different every time; when they get on stage they create a flow between the musicians that is unexplainable. A sound that is like no other and takes you on a musical journey. When a 'jam' happens all the instruments are bouncing off each other, and the crowd is so encased in that energy it is an experience you can get at no other show."
          —*Shauna T.*

"I actually despise the word jam band (well, not despise—dislike is a better word) because it could mean so many different genres nowadays—bluegrass, newgrass, dub-step, livetronica, psychedelic, traditional 'guitar-heavy' rock, world music, folk, cajun swampadelic, etc.—the term jam band is ambiguous and dated, as it has evolved from a Grateful Dead/New Riders–type world to a more all-inclusive term."
          —*Ryan N.*

"Jam band to me is the simple exploration of a thought, a cognitive journey through both the artist's and audience's minds (collective or singular) that begins in one realm, delves into another (and another and another) until it comes full circle in the end. When a band rips off into a stellar jam (solo or collaborative) one cannot help but feel transported out into the ether of their minds—literally showing us who we are, who they are, and what possibilities are out there."
          —*Michael P.*

"A jam band is a group of two or more musicians for whom play-ing—as opposed to singing, writing, or selling—music well is the highest priority."
                    —*Greg K.*

"Jam band to me is a band that goes off the beaten trail to find the sound and groove that connects the soul of the participants. The jam can begin by any one of the members and then finds its way to the rest of the band and then into the crowd. The crowd then becomes part of the band, and the music circulates throughout the entire space, creating a feeling of one. It must be a compila-tion of all the participants to achieve jam band status. This can be achieved in large settings or small intimate gatherings."
                    —*Tom M.*

"On one side of my brain, the term 'jam band' means pigeonhole. On the other side it means open-minded, open-ended freedom to explore the world of improvisation where no genre is out of bounds."
                    —*Keller W.*

"The musicians themselves seemed steeped in jazz and the art of improvisation. The whole Grateful Dead experience opened an-other world that you didn't hear on the radio. And not just what style they played or the shows, but it was an introduction to all of their influences. The covers they chose and the stuff they played during set breaks. That was my own true introduction to jazz, Rob-ert Johnson, old Appalachian traditional stuff, etc. I always felt that historical musical education was the greatest legacy of the Grateful Dead and Jerry Garcia. To me that was my favorite take-away beyond the fun times. And the success of the Dead then provided other musicians the confidence to pursue this form."
                    —*Jode J.*

"The term 'jam band' really describes the energy and vibe of the music/show experience before it explains anything else. All jam bands have a signature, something that makes them unique, but they all have a certain crackle of energy when seen live. They all lubricate the body and mind to overcome any anxiety of dancing like a freak in front of a large group of people or singing at the top of your lungs. When I hear the term 'jam band' I also tend to expect more from the music than I would of many other genres. I expect a certain hollow body guitar sound; I expect studio recordings to sound layered and complex and live recordings to take that song to a place that no one except for the musician could expect. You don't see bands just completely go off on a twenty-minute-long musical tangent, teasing other songs along the way, at any other shows. You don't see that type of improvisation at any type of show. That is unique to jam. And always will be."
                                                    —*Taylor W.*

What Does the Festival Scene Mean to You?

"Festivals are church for the open minded."
                                                    —*Jason M.*

"The festival scene is a special place to me. A festival to me is almost a quasi-religious/spiritual event in which people are all in unison with the music. The festival scene is a way of life that is about peace and unity through music, typically jam bands."
                                                    —*Michael A.*

"Community. An immersive shared experience of musical and personal discovery."
                                                    —*Eugene E.*

"The festival scene, to me, means freedom. Freedom from responsibility, freedom from electronic gadgets, freedom from worry. The festival scene means a collective gathering of kindred spirits to enjoy music and spend time together. For me, personally, it means a chance to spend quality time with my husband and focus on what's important in life—love."
—*Daisy H.*

"When I was younger the festival scene had a completely different feel and meaning to me. I watched the documentary called *tye-dyed*, where a camera crew followed the festival scene of Deadheads in '94. You can really see the difference between that scene and today's modern scene. There was such a strong family presence there, during the years of the Dead, where it was all about expressing oneself through the love of the art of music. Children grew up being submerged into this culture, and it was safe and kind. There are two festivals that I have been to, that really have stuck with me all this time. In 2005 I went to my last Bonnaroo Festival, and it was magical, but the following year learned that it had been bought out by a big name corporation and has become commercialized. Then in 2007 I went to a local festival in Atlanta, Georgia called the Echo Project. This festival was by far one of the best that I had experienced because it had that feel of the Dead followings in the nineties. All festivals today would like to say that they have that feel. However, more or less it's packed with trust-a-farians that are going for the sake of getting f-ed up on the drugs. Because they can only enjoy the show when they're geeked out. . . . or so they think. Music is an art, a way of life, a mediation and medicine for the soul. One that has a true understanding of the spiritual connection of music knows that music is the drug that submerges you into the soul of it. That's something that no drug can do."
—*Savanna C.*

"The scene is everything, or at least it used to be. It's sort of a coming-of-age phenomenon. It's dust for a young spirit's wanderlust. On a good day the scene is a Mecca of like-minded souls who gather and create and share and explore in unique togetherness. On a bad day it's a trap filled with addiction, chaos, fearful abandonment, and recklessness (wrecking-crew style). On an ordinary day it's just a parking lot or grass field filled with people who like to party and listen to music."

—*J. J. C.*

"Festivals are perhaps my favorite place on earth. The people that you meet there are possibly the greatest people that you could ever meet. Like Dead shows, the people at festivals are happy to see you and glad that you safely made it. I attended Philadelphia Folk Fest this year for the first time, and it made such an impression on me that I plan to go back every year. The vibes there were just so positive and beautiful. Also, camping with almost all of my closest friends was the absolute best way to spend a weekend at a festival. Festivals give me another reason to crave the summer and not go through winter."

—*Dylan B.*

"Festivals? Is this a true American collaboration of citizenry and a pure-hearted love of live art? Or a chance to party? A remnant of the Woodstock ethic of peace, love, and music? I guess a bit of everything is stoking the festival fires, and to me it's fantastic to see. Personally, I still get sick from a smorgasbord. I prefer my music and art in concentrated chunks that I can take in, rather than an offering of tons of bands over days and many stages, etc. It's too much for me to take in. But the trend the last twenty years toward all the festivals is giving musicians and fans a lifeline to perform and take in music in a safe and phenomenal way. Everybody seems pretty tweaked at festivals to me, so I see many folks use them as an opportunity to party, take some hallucinogens or whatever works for a long weekend, and the growth of the festivals these last few years is simply amazing, I think illustrating peoples need to be a part of something special. The power of collaboration and getting people together to feel good and be a part of something is important and not to just watch a bunch of overgrown steroid junkies kill each other on a football field or go to a church and praise some lord. This is special. Just ask the folks who go why they are going. Their answers are for the music, for what it feels like. The music is so powerful that the fans will go through a tremendous amount to make it happen. And so it becomes important and is a testament to how large amounts of Americans in the same place can actually be fun, amazing, and enlightening through our art. Music is truly the one language that reaches everyone, and its power through community has obviously become unmatched."

—*Todd W.*

"The festival scene to me can best be described as a place where peace and music, art and people collide to forge bonds that can be enjoyed in that moment in time. That enjoyment, those bonds can be easily rekindled and shared in the future at the next stop at the next festival."

—*Ross B.*

"The festival scene is a conglomeration of great and eclectic music, lots of friends and people who are like-minded, and always includes a great vending zone, or Shakedown Street, as we Dead-heads like to call it. A real family gathering around the thing we all love the most—the music!"

—*Randi M.*

"The festival scene to me is a place where people from all over the country/world/state can get together and share the same emotions and feelings about the bands there. It's a place to find out about new music and meet new people. Festivals create traditions between groups of friends and bring them closer to each other. People do crazy things and try crazy drugs, and your friends are there with you the whole time to experience it also. Festivals are a place for the weirdos to come out and be weird with no one watching."
—*Shauna T.*

"The festival scene is very important to me because of the camaraderie that I witness each festival I attend. Whether it be sharing with your neighbor, miracling someone, helping out someone who's 'in a bad spot,' or simply giving a stranger a hug, it solidifies my desire to introduce new people to the scene. One of my favorite things to do when covering a show is to get quotes from first-time festivarians to get their take on the experience. It helps me remember my first taste of this life—it makes me appreciate it all the more, as they witness happenings that we tend to take for granted, and you can tell that it will leave a lasting impression."
—*Ryan N.*

"As for the whole festival scene, though the amount of people attending can greatly influence how well the 'party' is received, it is a gathering of like-minded fans and 'explorers' who only want and need to be there. They are places to see old friends, make new ones, and live (if only for a few brief moments in time) the way man was intended to live. We are social creatures; the majority of the human race needs contact with other living beings, and festivals offer up that solution. Yes, the music plays a big part—let's face it, you wouldn't go if you didn't love the tunes—but it is the interaction between fans that makes it interesting. Everyone involved—vendors and patrons, security guards and assholes, and especially the band(s) and fans—are linked in a way that can only be described as symbiotic. As a whole we are there to revel in joy and celebrate a collective consciousness that can only come from being around like-minded (and hopefully peaceful) people. True, they can sometimes be overwhelming, and sometimes there are a few who disrupt the proceedings and generally disrespect the events going on, but those people may not have experienced the festival scene with the right frame of mind and attitudes associated with such gatherings. And even that is okay. There needs to be a balance—it is the law of nature. In the end it is more of what you take away from the festival than what you put in. And hopefully that is enough."

—*Michael P.*

"The festival scene, although I am not able to participate in it, represents a place where like-minded music lovers can gather and together reaffirm their appreciation and love of music of integrity and authenticity."

—*Greg K.*

"The festival scene to me means a gathering of peaceful philosophies converging onto a space that includes dance, art, crafts, food, natural surroundings, new acquaintances, and, most importantly, great music and lots of fun. It is like entering a Renaissance village of sorts with interesting people and a vibration that can be felt by all who choose to participate."

—*Tom M.*

"The festival scene is a utopian community that has the ability to rise above any weather condition with its masterful outdoor survival skills. It's a pleasant troop of folks that share a common bond of love for music, camping, and the all-night rager."

—*Keller W.*

"Festivals, namely jazz/folk/bluegrass, have been around for a long time. The current 'jam band' festival scene was a natural succession to Dead, particularly after '95. It filled a void. And for many it was an introduction to new bands and new music. Without those festivals there was very little opportunity for a lot of musicians to be heard."

—*Jode J.*

"The festival scene is the reason I work all year round at a job I hate. It's my main priority, really. I save all year to go to festivals. I feel at home there. Festivals are the one place that I feel I can truly be myself. For someone stuck at a corporation and that has non–jam band fan friends, it's quite the release. The festival scene means, above all things, community. You meet these people, talk to them for either the entire festival or just for a few minutes, exchange contact info sometimes, exchange a cool shirt for a cool pin or whatever, and then that little heartfelt meeting is with you forever. You either keep in contact with these people or you have something that was theirs. It's an odd concept to people outside of the scene. It's odd for someone who doesn't see that type of kindness and openness in everyday life. People don't get it. They look at me and say, 'So you're going to drive to another state, camp out for four days without a shower or even a cot, surrounded by strangers, just to listen to music?' And then you have to say, 'Well, it's Furthur, so yeah.' And they still don't get it. The festival scene is so esoteric. And it will always be that way. Because these bands capture our hearts and make us feel like we have purpose. They move us with their music. They make us travel to the ends of the earth, sleep on the ground, pretty much anything to see these bands. And no one else will ever understand. And we like it that way."

—*Taylor W.*

Contributor Notes

*Every musician noted here has played in various bands throughout their career and many have active side projects (sometimes multiple active side projects). For the purposes of these notes I have focused on listing the bands with which each artist is most typically associated and/or those most relevant to this book.
—*P. C.*

Andrew Altman plays upright bass in Railroad Earth.

Vinnie Amico plays drums in moe.

Trey Anastasio is best known as guitarist, lead singer, primary songwriter, and founding member of Phish.

Chris Barron is lead singer and founding member of the Spin Doctors.

John Bell plays rhythm guitar and is lead vocalist for Widespread Panic.

Marco Benevento is a pianist, organist, composer, and cofounder of the Royal Potato Family music label.

Jay Blakesberg is a photographer and filmmaker best known for his live concert photos and portraits of bands and musicians.

Tim Bluhm plays guitar and is a lead vocalist for the Mother Hips.

Dean Budnick is a writer, filmmaker, and historian. He is founder of jambands.com, cofounder of the Jammy Awards, and executive editor of *Relix* magazine.

Larry Campbell is a multi-instrumentalist who has played and toured extensively with Bob Dylan and served as musical director and band leader for Levon Helm's Midnight Rambles. He has played on numerous recordings by the country's top artists in multiple genres.

Tim Carbone plays violin and sings vocals in Railroad Earth.

Justin Carrey plays bass and is a founding member of the Heavy Pets.

Tom Constanten is a composer and keyboardist best known for playing with the Grateful Dead from 1968 to 1970.

Joel Cummins is keyboardist, vocalist, and founding member of Umphrey's McGee.

Rob Derhak plays bass and is a founding member of moe.

Rob Eaton plays guitar and is a lead vocalist in Dark Star Orchestra. He is also a sound engineer who began his career as one of the original tapers in the Grateful Dead scene.

Dino English is a drummer in Dark Star Orchestra.

Alan Evans is drummer and founding member of Soulive. He was also a founding member of Moon Boot Lover.

Perry Farrell is lead singer in Jane's Addiction and founder of Lollapalooza.

John Fishman is a drummer and sings vocals in Phish.

Béla Fleck is a banjo player best known for his work in Béla Fleck and the Flecktones.

David Gans is a journalist, musician, producer, author, and host of the weekly syndicated radio show *The Grateful Dead Hour* and cohost of the radio show *Tales from the Golden Road* on the Grateful Dead channel on Sirius/XM.

Chuck Garvey is guitarist and a founding member of moe.

Reid Genaur plays guitar and is lead vocalist and founding member of Assembly of Dust. He was also a founding member of Strangefolk.

Andy Goessling plays acoustic guitars, banjo, dobro, mandolin, flute, pennywhistle, and saxophones and sings vocals in Railroad Earth.

David Graham has worked as a band manager (most notably for Blues Traveler) and concert promoter and was pivotal in such festivals as the Arrowhead Ranch concerts and the H.O.R.D.E. tour. He serves on the board of the Bill Graham Memorial Foundation, named in honor of his father, the concert promoter Bill Graham.

Jackie Greene is a singer-songwriter best known for his work as a solo musician. His recent projects and collaborations include playing with such musicians as Bob Weir, Phil Lesh, Joan Osborne, and Chris Robinson.

Jon Gutwillig is guitarist and founding member of the Disco Biscuits.

Col. Bruce Hampton is an innovative guitarist, vocalist, and songwriter whose bands include the Aquarium Rescue Unit, the Code Talkers, and the Hampton Grease Band.

Carey Harmon plays drums and hand percussion and sings vocals in Railroad Earth.

Mickey Hart is a percussionist and musicologist best known for his work as drummer in the Grateful Dead.

Ken Hayes is founder of the Gathering of the Vibes music festival and former owner of Terrapin Tapes, a media distribution outlet for tapers and tape traders.

Warren Haynes is a guitarist, vocalist, songwriter, and founding member of Gov't Mule. He has also notably played with the Allman Brothers, the Dead, and Phil Lesh and Friends, and he maintains a solo career.

Jo Jo Hermann is keyboardist, sings vocals, and is a founding member of Widespread Panic.

Jimmy Herring is lead guitarist in Widespread Panic. He has also notably played in Aquarium Rescue Unit, the Allman Brothers Band, Derek Trucks Band, the Dead, and with Phil Lesh and Friends.

Jeff Howard plays guitar and sings vocals in the McLovins.

Jake Huffman is drummer and sings vocals in the McLovins.

Michael Kang plays mandolin, sings vocals, and is a founding member of the String Cheese Incident.

Dan Keller plays guitar and sings vocals in Giant Panda Guerilla Dub Squad.

Steve Kimock is a guitarist, songwriter, and founder of the Steve Kimock Band. He has notably played with Zero and contributed to solo projects by various members of the Grateful Dead.

Rob Koritz is a drummer in Dark Star Orchestra.

Eric Krasno is guitarist, sings vocals, and is a founding member of Soulive.

Bill Kreutzmann is best known as drummer and founding member of the Grateful Dead. His most recent band is 7 Walkers.

Chris Kuroda is lighting director for the band Phish.

Jeff Lloyd plays guitar and sings vocals in the Heavy Pets.

Greg Loiacono plays guitar and is a lead vocalist in the Mother Hips.

Jim Loughlin plays percussion in moe.

Aron Magner plays keyboards and is a founding member of the Disco Biscuits.

Taj Mahal is a singer-songwriter, guitarist, and legendary blues musician.

Papa Mali plays guitar, sings lead vocals, and is a founding member of 7 Walkers.

Jono Manson is a music producer, singer-songwriter, guitar player, and founding member of the Worms.

Jeff Mattson plays guitar and is a lead vocalist in Dark Star Orchestra. He is also a founding member of the Zen Tricksters and has played with the Donna Jean Godchaux Band and Phil Lesh and Friends.

John Medeski is a keyboard player, composer, and founding member of Medeski, Martin and Wood.

Mark Mercier plays keyboards and sings vocals in Max Creek.

Horace Moore is archivist for Widespread Panic.

Keith Mosley plays bass, sings vocals, and is a founding member of the String Cheese Incident.

Scott Murawski is guitar player and lead vocalist in Max Creek. He has also notably played in side projects with Mike Gordon and Bill Kreutzmann.

Ivan Neville is a singer, songwriter, keyboardist, vocalist, and founding member of Dumpstaphunk. He has also notably played with the Neville Brothers and with Keith Richards.

Tara Nevins is a multi-instrumentalist, a lead vocalist, and founding member of Donna the Buffalo.

Zach Newton has worked as stage manager, sound engineer, and in other capacities for such bands as Aquarium Rescue Unit, Widespread Panic, and, most recently, Béla Fleck and the Flecktones.

Jason Ott plays bass, sings vocals, and is a founding member of the McLovins.

Stephen Perkins is a drummer, percussionist, and founding member of Jane's Addiction. His solo band is Banyan.

John Popper plays harmonica, sings lead vocals, and is a founding member of Blues Traveler. He played a seminal role in the founding of the H.O.R.D.E. Festival.

George Porter Jr. is bassist, sings vocals, and is a founding member of the Meters, a band often credited as one of the progenitors of funk.

Jeb Puryear plays guitar, sings vocals, and is a founding member of Donna the Buffalo.

Parke Puterbaugh is a music journalist and author whose books include *Phish: The Biography*.

Tim Reynolds is a songwriter and guitarist who has played extensively with the Dave Matthews Band and as one half of the Dave Matthews–Tim Reynolds duo. He is founding member of TR3.

John Rider plays bass, sings vocals, and is a founding member of Max Creek.

Stephen Robinson was percussionist for Jabez Stone.

Joe Russo is a drummer and founding member of the Benevento/Russo Duo. He has notably served as drummer in Furthur and such other bands as Fat Mama, Robert Walter's 20th Congress, and in a side project with Trey Anastasio, Mike Gordon, and Marco Benevento.

Dylan Savage plays guitar, sings vocals, and is a founding member of Giant Panda Guerilla Dub Squad.

Al Schnier plays guitar and sings vocals in moe.

Dave Schools plays bass and is a founding member of Widespread Panic.

James Searl plays bass, sings vocals, and is a founding member of Giant Panda Guerilla Dub Squad.

Peter Shapiro is a music impresario whose contributions include owning/operating Wetlands Preserve, Brooklyn Bowl, and the Capitol Theatre. He is also publisher of *Relix* magazine and cofounder of the Jammy Awards.

John Skehan plays mandolin and sings vocals in Railroad Earth.

Amy Skelton is widely credited as being Phish's first fan.

Michael Travis is drummer and founding member of the String Cheese Incident. He currently plays in the electronic music band EOTO.

Mick Vaughn plays bass in TR3.

Bob Weir is a guitar player, vocalist, songwriter, and founding member of the Grateful Dead. Most recently he created Tamalpais Research Institute (TRI Studios), a state-of-the-art video streaming venue and recording facility.

Keller Williams is a singer-songwriter and multi-instrumentalist best known as a solo performer.

I Want to Thank You . . .

I hesitate to even start a "thank you" list for this book because so many people have helped in so many ways, large and small, along the way. For instance, what is the name of that smiling security guard at Gathering of the Vibes who danced a jig with me outside the media tent, reminding me that, despite any runarounds while trying to get interviews, it was all about the music? Thanks for the dance, brother. There were literally thousands of such people—musicians, fans, crew members, promoters, security, random people in convenience stores, and so forth—who made this project a pleasure, an adventure, and a reminder of how the music, travel, and camaraderie of the jam scene is what keeps us all coming back year after year. Wherever and whoever you are—thank you all.

It is virtually impossible to imagine working on *JAMerica* without Denver Miller and J. R. Kraus. Along with writing this book, Denver, J. R., and I have been working on a documentary film version of *JAMerica*. We made this entire trip together—and had an absolute blast doing it. You guys have been amazing partners and brothers in arms. I thank you for agreeing to "share the ride" as a trio and look forward to bringing your amazing footage to the JAMerican public. I'd also like to note that due to conflicts with my schedule, Denver and J. R. conducted the interview with Stephen Perkins, and J. R. conducted the interview with Perry Ferrell without me being present—I thank them for allowing me to use those interviews in this book. Also instrumental in the *JAMerica* documentary film project are Steve Smock, our graphic design/website/artist in residence, and William "Shack" Shackleton, who helped with several interviews.

Each interview in this book had to be transcribed before sections of it could be inserted into the "discussion." I had early help on that transcribing from Gina Caciolo, Heather Cortright, and Erin Parker, and I thank them all for helping me get this project off the ground. The bulk of the transcription was done by Amanda Fantauzzo, who juggled this work while raising her own two girls and being a nanny (and, often, life—and sanity—saver) for my family. Thank you, Amanda, for your hard work, enthusiasm, and special friendship—you rock.

None of these interviews would have been possible without the assistance of all the publicists and tour managers who work their asses off to bring the artists, who then bring the music, to us. After writing this book I have a newfound—and profound—respect for all the people who make the shows possible. They do more than we dancing fools in the audience can ever imagine. Thanks to all of you who helped with scheduling and support along the way. Special thanks to Carrie Lombardi at Madison House Publicity and Erin Scholze at Dream Spider Publicity, who helped secure some crucial early interviews with String Cheese Incident and Keller Williams (Carrie) and Donna the Buffalo (Erin) that helped us find our feet and get the project rolling. Both Carrie and Erin have continued to help along the way too, and on behalf of Denver and J. R., we are grateful for all you've done and continue to do.

Despite my statement in the Preface that jam bands are not "camera friendly," it must be acknowledged that the photos in this book are amazing. Each photographer generously donated their work and, in so doing, enriched it greatly. My thanks to them all. Thanks, too, to Danielle DiNatale of Dee Marie Photography for my shiny new author photos.

Thank you to Steve Silberman, who sat with me in his apartment in San Francisco while I fumbled through a list of potential book titles and then, in a flash of brilliance, called out, "Jamerica!" The title was a lock as soon as it came out of Steve's mouth. I'm proud to wave that flag.

Writers dream of having an editor who believes in their vision and truly "gets" why they feel passionate about a project. I have such an editor in Ben Schafer. Ben brought me into the Da Capo Press fold with the publication of my book *Growing Up Dead,* and when *JAMerica* was proposed he recognized immediately why a book documenting the jam band scene was important (even turning over his office to us for an interview with David Graham). He has been a dream editor, advocate, and, I'm proud to say, friend. Thank you, Ben. And thank you to all the hardworking crew at Da Capo Press (especially Kate Burke, Sean Maher, and Cisca Schreefel), who labor to put my writing into your hands.

My agent, Linda Roghaar, of the Linda Roghaar Literary Agency, has believed in my writing since well before any publishers were on board. In fact, longer, perhaps, than either one of us would care to acknowledge. She's helped me grow, progress, find my voice, and—what the hell?—make a few bucks in the process. Thank you, Linda, for believing in me all these years.

The *JAMerica* crew made its way into many venues to conduct these interviews (no small task when you're talking about making room for a film crew as opposed to a single writer with a handheld recorder), and by and large, those venues have been more than gracious. I'd particularly like to thank John Chmiel and his staff at Rochester, New York's own Water Street Music Hall, where we conducted more interviews than anywhere else. Thanks also to the Rochester local music venues Abilene Bar and Lounge (special thanks to Danny Deutsch), Harro East Ballroom, the Auditorium Theater, and the German House. On the festival front, Ken Hayes and Jonathan Healey welcomed *JAMerica* to the Gathering of the Vibes for two consecutive years while these interviews were being conducted and provided a model for how a stellar jam festival should run. You guys are the best. I'd also like to give a special thank you to Bob Weir, Justin Kreutzmann, Chris McCutcheon, and the whole crew at TRI Studios, who hosted us for multiple days and interviews. TRI is working the cutting edge of broadcasting intimate live shows—and having a blast doing it. Thanks for including us in the fun.

There are people who serve as the gatekeepers to any given scene because they have earned the trust and respect of those around them. Many of those people gave us interviews but, equally importantly, helped open doors to their colleagues by giving us the thumbs-up. Those people include Keller Williams, Tara Nevins, David Gans, David Graham, Mark Pinkus, Brad Tucker, Peter Shapiro, Tommy Brunett, Doug Goodman, Steve Silbermann, Dean Budnick, Dan "The Doctor" Smith, and dozens of other people who—though I apologize for not listing your names here—know who you are. Huge thanks also to my brother-for-life Todd Weiner and Robb's Boulder Music for opening their doors to us in Boulder, Colorado, and also surprising me with the gift of a recorder that I used for these interviews.

Thank you to BOA Editions, Ltd.—where I proudly serve as publisher—for granting me the time and space I need to continue my writing and for supporting those efforts with enthusiasm. Special thanks to my coworkers and friends Melissa Hall and Jenna Fuller for your camaraderie and good spirits.

Although it goes without saying, this book wouldn't have happened if the musicians hadn't given of their time to sit down for these interviews—and often allow us to film their shows. I am constantly astounded by your passion for your music and your dedication to your fans. Heartfelt thanks to all of you who consented to speak your minds in these pages.

And, of course, I save the most important "thank you" for last. To my wife, Karen, who has believed in my writing from day one . . . who held down the fort with our three kids while I was running around the country to all these shows . . . who somehow juggles being a brilliant psychologist, a loving wife, and an amazing mother all at the same time . . . who constantly inspires and amazes me—I love you. And to my kids, Whitman, Max, and Kane, who were so patient as their dad hit the road and always made coming back home feel like Christmas morning (even when I wasn't able to bring them back a present). I love you all.

Acknowledgments

Thank you to the following magazines, publishers, and writers whose excerpts appear in these pages. *Asterisk indicates permission is still forthcoming.*

Magazine and Website Acknowledgments

*Baca, Ricardo, "Interview: The Disco Biscuits," Heyreverb.com, May 28, 2009.

*Bell, John, *Georgia*, March 2010.

Berk, Jamie, "Interview with Jon Gutwillig," *Dartmouth Independent*, June 17, 2012.

*Bonyata, Phil, "A Musician's Musician: Livewire's Exclusive Interview with Allman Brothes Band and Gov't Mule's Warren Haynes," Concertlivewire.com, September 13, 2007.

Budnick, Dean, "H.O.R.D.E. 20 Years On," *Relix*, April 4, 2012.

*Castro, Chris, "Interview with the Disco Biscuits: Always on Time," *Aquarian Weekly*, December 23, 2009.

Calemine, James, "Sage and Spirit from Widespread Panic's John Bell . . . 25 years of Music and Musings," *Swampland*.

Calemine, James, "Walking with Zambi: The Colonel Bruce Hampton Interview," *Swampland*.

*Chesham, Jake, "The High Times Interview: Trey Anastasio," *High Times*, June 13, 2002.

*Collette, Doug, "Jackie Greene: The Prince of Americana," *Glide*, April 14, 2008.

*Hansen, Liane, "Interview with Composer Ernie Stires with Trey Anastasio," NPR's *Weekend Edition*, December 20, 1998.

Harriman, Bill, "m.o.e.," Swaves.com, June 2006.

Humphrey, Michelle, "Exclusive Interview with Jimmy Herring," Examiner.com, August 14, 2012.

"Interview: Al Schnier from moe.," *Headcount*, April 17, 2012.

*"Interview with Jimmy Herring," *Digital Interviews*, May 1999.

Johnson, McClain, "Interview: Horace Moore, WSP Archivist," *Bands That Jam*, July 7, 2011.

Johnson, McClain, "Interview: Jo Jo Hermann," Gonola.com, August 12, 2009.

Johnson, McClain, "George Porter, Jr.: Interview with a Legendary New Orleans Musician," Gonola.com, November 11, 2010.

Kessinger, Kent, "Interview with John Medeski of Medeski, Martin and Wood," Nowpublic.com, April 1, 2009.

Lockwood, Jeff.,"Interview: moe. Vinnie Amico (Drummer)," Inmusicwetrust.com, December 4, 2012.

Murphy, Robert, "Interview with Warren Haynes," *Murf's Southern Steel*, April 7, 1998.

*Rose, Charlie, "Conversation with Phish Frontman Trey Anastasio," *Charlie Rose*, August 6, 2004.

Simonini, Ross, "Interview with Trey Anastasio," *The Believer*, July/August 2011.

*Snyder, Michael, "Interview with Trey," posted on Gadiel.com.

*Varian, Ethan, "Jimmy Herring Discusses Influences and Incorporating Outside Sounds Into His Playing," *Guitar World*, November 1, 2011.

*Wasilczuk, Madalyn, "Jam Bands Rock New York," *The Eagle*, December 6, 2006.

"What Is the Phish and Band Member Official Taping Policy?," Phish.com.

Book Acknowledgments

Brown, Toni, "An Interview with Bob Weir," *Relix: The Book*, Backbeat Books, 2009.

Goldberg, Matt, "The Great American H.O.R.D.E.," *Relix: The Book*, Backbeat Books, 2009.

Mullen, Brendan, *Whores: An Oral Biography of Perry Farrell and Jane's Addiction*, Da Capo Press, 2005.

*Phish and Richard Gehr, *The Phish Book*, Villard, 1998.

Puterbaugh, Parke, *Phish: The Biography*, Da Capo Press, 2009.

Index

About the Author

PETER CONNERS is author of the memoir *Growing Up Dead: The Hallucinated Confessions of a Teenage Deadhead* and the nonfiction study *White Hand Society: The Psychedelic Partnership of Timothy Leary and Allen Ginsberg*. His other books include the prose poetry collections *Of Whiskey and Winter* and *The Crows Were Laughing in Their Trees*, the novella *Emily Ate the Wind*, and *PP/FF: An Anthology* (editor). He lives in Rochester, New York, where he works as publisher of the not-for-profit literary press BOA Editions.